U.S Fish & Wildlife Service

A Guide to Nestling Development and Aging in Altricial Passerines

Biological Technical Publication

BTP-R6008-2007

U.S Fish & Wildlife Service

A Guide to Nestling Development and Aging in Altricial Passerines

Biological Technical Publication

BTP-R6008-2007

Dennis Jongsomjit[1]

Stephanie L. Jones[2]

Thomas Gardali[1]

Geoffrey R. Geupel[1]

Paula J. Gouse[3]

[1] PRBO Conservation Science, Petaluma, CA

[2] U.S. Fish and Wildlife Service, Region 6, Office of Migratory Birds, Denver, CO

[3] U.S. Fish and Wildlife Service, Bowdoin National Wildlife Refuge, Malta, MT

Cover images: Top: Crissal Thrasher, *Toxostoma crissale*
Bottom: Brewer's Sparrow, *Spizella breweri*

Photo credits: Top: Chris McCreedy/PRBO
Bottom: Colin Wooley/PRBO

AUTHOR CONTACT INFORMATION:
Dennis Jongsomjit
PRBO Conservation Science
3820 Cypress Drive
Petaluma, CA 94954
707-781-2555
email:djongsomjit@prbo.org

Stephanie L. Jones
U.S. Fish and Wildlife Service, Region 6
Nongame Migratory Birds
P.O. Box 25486 DFC
Denver, CO 80225
303-236-4409
Email: stephanie_jones@fws.gov

Thomas Gardali
PRBO Conservation Science
3820 Cypress Drive
Petaluma, CA 94954
415-868-0655 x 381
Email: tgardali@prbo.org

Geoffrey R. Geupel
PRBO Conservation Science
3820 Cypress Drive
Petaluma, CA 94954
415-868-0655 x 301
Email: ggeupel@prbo.org

Paula J. Gouse
U.S. Fish and Wildlife Service
Bowdoin National Wildlife Refuge
194 Bowdoin Auto Tour Rd
Malta, MT 59538
406-654-2863
Email: paula_gouse@fws.gov

FOR ADDITIONAL COPIES OR INFORMATION CONTACT:
U.S. Fish and Wildlife Service, Region 6
Nongame Migratory Bird Program
P.O. Box 25486 DFC
Denver, CO 80225-0486

RECOMMENDED CITATION:
Jongsomjit, D., S. L. Jones, T. Gardali, G. R. Geupel, and P. J. Gouse. 2007. A guide to nestling development and aging in altricial passerines. U.S. Department of Interior, Fish and Wildlife Service, Biological Technical Publication, FWS/BTP-R6008-2007, Washington, D.C.

Table of Contents

List of Figures

Acknowledgments

The collection of data for this guide would not have been possible without the help of many interns and field biologists including Parvaneh C. Abbaspour, Bethany S. Atchley, Amon J. Armstrong, Ross R. Conover, Gerhard A. Epke, Tristan R. Gingerich, Geetha M. Jayabose, Scott F. Jennings, Laura H. Kaplan, Errin B. Kramer-Wilt, Ben G. Larson, Blaine MacDonald, Emily Morrison, Henry Ndithia, Kerry E. Neijstrom, Alexander Rosenthal, Corrina Snow, Amanda B. Shults, and Dionne R. Wrights. Many thanks to Suzanne Austin-Blythell, Bruce Barbour, Thomas M. Haggerty, Steve N. G. Howell, and Diana L. Humple for providing helpful comments to earlier drafts of this guide. Fig. 1 is adapted from Gill (1994) and Fig. 6 is adapted from Baldwin et al. (1931). We thank Peter Pyle and Steve N. G. Howell for graciously allowing us the use of Figs. 2, 3, and 5 (Pyle 1997). Figures 4, 7, and 8 were drawn by Dennis Jongsomjit. We thank the Point Reyes National Seashore for their continued cooperation. Funding was provided by the U.S. Fish and Wildlife Service Region 6 Nongame Migratory Bird Program. This is PRBO contribution 1603.

Data Contributors
We especially thank the colleagues that contributed nestling data to this publication: Ryan Burnett and Vanessa Tissdale – PRBO Conservation Science, Dusky Flycatcher *(Empidonax oberholseri)* and Thomas M. Haggerty – Department of Biology, University of North Alabama, Carolina Wren *(Thryothorus ludovicianus)*.

Introduction

Nestling growth and development studies have been a topic of interest for a greater part of the last century (Sutton 1935, Walkinshaw 1948) and continue to be of interest today. This is not surprising since studies on nestling growth can provide a wealth of biological information that has larger implications for avian management and conservation. Despite this history of studying nestling development, basic information is still limited or absent for many species. Many questions remain unanswered, and contradictory conclusions are often found in the literature (Starck and Ricklefs 1998a). Therefore, much information on aging and development can still be gained from studying the development patterns of similar species and from comparative studies, across avian orders (Minea et al. 1982, Saunders and Hansen 1989, Carsson and Hörnfeldt 1993). Additionally, nestling growth studies can yield insight into the effects of different nesting strategies on productivity (O'Connor 1978), as well as the impacts of parental effort and environmental variables on fitness (Ross 1980, Ricklefs and Peters 1981, Magrath 1991). Since low reproductive success may play a significant role in the declines of many North American passerines (Sherry and Holmes 1992, Ballard et al. 2003), a better understanding of the factors that influence reproductive success is a vital component of avian conservation (Martin 1992). Data on nestling aging can be used to improve nest survival estimates (Dinsmore 2002, Nur et al. 2004), providing information that can be used to more precisely age nests (Pinkowski 1975, Podlesack and Blem 2002), (Jones and Geupel 2007). Indeed, the relatively short time period young spend developing in the nest is a critical part of a bird's life cycle and a nestling's developmental path can affect its survival to independence, its survival as an adult, and its future reproductive success.

Nestling Growth

Ornithologists categorize birds over an altricial to precocial spectrum, based on differences in the rate of growth and type of development young birds will undertake (Starck and Ricklefs 1998b). Placement into this spectrum depends on various broad characteristics such as mobility, feeding behavior, presence of down, and parental nest attendance (Gill 1994). Growth rates are highly variable within the altricial to precocial spectrum, with developmental periods varying as much as 30-fold (Ricklefs 1983). Much of this variation in growth can be attributed, at the phylogenetic level, to differences in body mass. In general, altricial species can grow at 3-4 times the rate of precocial species, and growth rates of birds with similar mass can vary by as much as a factor of 10 (Ricklefs et al. 1998). In this guide, we focus on altricial species.

Nestling growth variability has largely been studied looking at effects on individual fitness of offspring and parents (e.g., Murphy 1983, Magrath 1991, Halupka 1998). Differences between populations can manifest as morphological differences or differential timing in the growth and maturation of certain body components (Murphy 1983, Burns 1993). However, the growth rate of a single species throughout its entire range can sometimes vary little (King and Hubbard 1981, Murphy 1983, Pereyra and Morton 2001).

Variability in nestling growth rates can be due to many ecological factors, in conjunction with specific species life history strategies; some developmental processes might be linked and are also independent of the nutritional state of a nestling (Ricklefs 1968a). Some factors associated with species specific growth rates and patterns include nest location, synchronicity of hatching, and brood size (Murphy 1983). Ecological factors that influence nestling growth are generally related to limitations in food availability (Ricklefs 1993), including weather (Petersen et al. 1986), habitat differences and quality (Ross 1980, Dawson and Bidwell 2005), parasites (Burhans et al. 2000), competition between nest mates (Werschkul and Jackson 1979, Ricklefs 1982), and parental abilities (Briskie 1995). Additionally, higher nest-predation rates may favor higher nestling growth rates (Lack 1968, Remes and Martin 2002, but see Ricklefs 1969).

At the physiological level, an important factor thought to limit growth is "tissue level constraint", where nestlings are growing at a maximum rate allowable by the tradeoff existing between resources available for growth and mature tissue function (Ricklefs et al. 1998). Once certain types of cells differentiate into mature functioning tissue, they no longer continue to grow (O'Connor 1984). After a period of below normal growth, a nestling would need to increase its growth rate in order to "catch up" to its normal developmental timing. However, such compensatory growth has not been shown to occur in altricial birds (Schew and Ricklefs 1998, Lepczyk and Karasov 2000; but see Remes and Martin 2002, Bize et al. 2006). In one study, addition of body mass and growth rates in overfed young in the laboratory did not differ from that of wild young

(Konarzewski et al.1996). These results indicate that young may be growing at the maximum rate allowed by cell function and physiology.

Analyzing Growth

An important part of visualizing and analyzing nestling growth is the use of fitted growth equations (Ricklefs 1967, 1983). When fitted into a growth equation, using non-linear regression, three components of growth are provided: the rate, magnitude, and form of growth. When graphed, nestling growth is often shown to increase, reach a peak, and finally level off in a sigmoidal shape. These equations simplify and allow for comparative analysis of growth between and within species. Information on adult body weight and size are also an important aspect of analyzing growth with these equations (O'Connor 1984); adult body size measurements are provided for the study species in this guide (Appendix A). Alternatively, growth data can also be used to build predictive models of age (Holcomb and Twiest 1971, Hamel 1974).

Growth Patterns and Aging

Inherent species specific patterns of growth and development can often be used to age nestlings (Starck and Ricklefs 1998a). In nestling growth patterns, each body component can begin growth at a different point in time relative to other components, resulting in a staggered growth pattern. Specific patterns in this type of growth are generally adaptations for nest survival. For example, in some species, contour feathers tend to rapidly grow and unsheathe before the remiges, providing important insulation cover early in life, when young cannot self-thermoregulate (Murphy 1981). In another example, growth of the tarsus or gape, important for food acquisition, may proceed rapidly during the early nestling stage (O'Connor 1984). Besides growth, developmental events (e.g., pin-feather eruption patterns, eye opening, and behavior) can be age specific and are readily observed (Ricklefs 1966, Murphy 1981). Thus, using a combination of several growth measurements can provide reliable aging throughout the nestling period (King and Hubbard 1981, Murphy 1981, Haggerty 1994, Podlesak and Blem 2002).

Aging Recommendations

The type and number of measurements needed for reliable aging may vary among species but preliminary analysis of our data shows that wing length, tarsus length, weight, and culmen provide good predictive models of age. Since nestlings may be growing at a maximized rate, age estimates can be informed by considering the development of the most advanced nestlings, and by using more than one nestling. In nests parasitized by Brown-headed Cowbird *(Molothrus ater)*, where all the young may be receiving less food than normal, aging host young may or may not be reliable (Kilner et al. 2004, Weatherhead 1989). Aging of the Brown-headed Cowbird young may be possible, depending on the host species (Scott 1979, Kilpatric 2002).

With any aging technique, it is important to be aware that deviations from normal growth and development can occur, preventing accurate predictions of age for those individuals. Data from known age nests can bring attention to abnormal developmental patterns and rates in the local populations. Measuring nestlings on more than one day can also reveal deviations from normal development. Energy restrictions can be a source of another type of staggered growth where nestlings are forced to allocate resources to areas of development more important to their survival (Oyan and Anker-Nilssen 1996, Dahdul and Horn 2003). This could result in some body components growing normally, while others slow or stop growing completely (Boag 1987, Lepczyk and Karasov 2000). Feather developmental events in particular, such as pin feather eruption, may proceed normally, despite abnormal growth in other body components (Schew and Ricklefs 1998). Hence, though measuring several variables may help reduce aging error, if any abnormal patterns are identified individuals should be aged with caution.

Variables Used for Aging

Several measurements of growth have been widely used in the literature. We have attempted to be as inclusive as possible with the variables used in this guide. Given the time restrictions of measuring young, we have narrowed the variables to those that proved useful in the literature and in field trials.

Individual feather tracts.—The developmental timing of feather tracts tends to follow a consistent age related pattern within a species and are the most easily noted traits when examining nestlings. The flight feathers will often begin to emerge and develop in pin before the contour feathers; however, contour feathers will often begin to unsheathe before the flight feathers (Murphy 1981). Feather development may proceed independently of growth in body size or mass gain (Ricklefs 1968a). These qualities make feather development an important component of aging nestlings.

Wing Chord.—Wing chord is another simple measurement that is reported often in the literature. As part of staggered development, wing growth can proceed quickly throughout the nestling stage and has been shown to provide a good estimate of age (Ricklefs 1975, Haggerty 1994, McCarty 2001).

Weight.—Data on mass gain is the most common data published on nestling growth. This may be, in part, because it is a relatively easy measurement to take. Though nestlings may gain mass at rapid levels, mass gain may be more sensitive than other parameters to food availability or environmental stress and may not always reflect the maturity level of a nestling (Boag 1987, Lepczyk and Karasov 2000). In some species, such as aerial foragers and cavity nesters, mass may even reach an asymptotic peak above normal adult weight, and then diminish to normal levels before fledging (Ricklefs 1968b). For these reasons, mass should not be used alone to indicate age. Nevertheless, its wide availability in the literature makes mass a practical component of nestling aging.

Tarsus.—Tarsus length may grow normally even with food restrictions (Best 1977, Lepczyk and Karasov 2000). The tarsus is also a part of the staggered development seen in nestlings. For example, in the Bachman's Sparrow (*Aimophila aestivalis*), the tarsus was shown to grow quickly during the early part of the nestling stage before tapering off after day 5 (Haggerty 1994).

Primary and rectrix pin lengths.—Flight feather growth proceeds quickly and may be affected by factors different from those that affect mass gain (Murphy 1985). Also, growth of the remiges may not be as erratic as weight gain, making it a more-reliable age indicator (King and Hubbard 1981, Boag 1987). While primary pins usually grow rapidly, in some species this growth may begin to slow down and in some cases length may reach a maximum late in the nestling period. Rectrices, on the other hand, usually do not begin to develop until the latter half of the nestling period, where they proceed to grow rapidly. This division in growth schedule allows one to measure rapidly growing flight feathers throughout the nestling stage.

Culmen.—The culmen can serve as a good age indicator since it may grow normally despite food restrictions (Lepczyk and Karasov 2000). For many species, the culmen is also a relatively simple measurement to take.

Eyes.—Nestlings will often begin to open their eyes at a predictable age. Thus, this event can serve to reinforce age estimates. The date the eyes begin to open is especially useful, while the degree of eye opening can vary considerably.
Longest broken primary.—The degree of exposed primary feather is a development process that may proceed independent of growth and can be used to reinforce nestling age estimates.

Total length.—Total length is historically an important standard measurement (Baldwin et al. 1931) that is relatively simple and quick to take. However, the length can increase quickly, and should be used with caution. The position of the young can reduce or increase this measurement dramatically.

Gape and rictus.—The gape can grow quickly early in the nestling period. However, the rictus (soft tissue at base of bill) is very pliable during growth, and measurements of the gape can increase or decrease greatly between days as the rictus contracts and expands. Hence, it should be both measured and used with caution.

Physical and behavioral descriptors.—Because certain behavioral events can consistently occur at a specific age and are easily noted (Ricklefs 1966), they are an important part of aging the young. They can also prove useful in narrowing age determination when growth data places the age of the nestling within a certain range.

Yellow-breasted chat (Icteria virens). Chris McCreedy/PRBO

Objectives

We had two primary objectives in writing this guide, to report and promote research on species specific patterns of altricial passerine nestling development and aging, and to achieve better estimates of nestling ages. We present nestling data on seven species of altricial passerines: Dusky Flycatcher *(Empidonax oberholseri)*, Carolina Wren *(Thryothorus ludovicianus)*, Wrentit *(Chamea fasciata)*, Sprague's Pipit *(Anthus spragueii)*, Song Sparrow *(Melospiza melodia)*, Chestnut-collared Longspur *(Calcarius ornatus)*, and American Goldfinch *(Cardeulis tristis)*. In addition, nestling data collection techniques have been highly variable, limiting the potential for data sharing, limiting comparisons across species and families, and limiting the use of data in combined analyses. Therefore, we present suggestions for standardizing the collection of nestling data in Appendix B.

Methods

Using the Species Accounts

In the species accounts we report detailed information on species-specific nestling development. A primary goal in the design of the accounts was to make them as useful as possible for those interested in aging nestlings. The first page of each account begins with life history information for the particular species. This is followed immediately by tables listing distinguishing developmental criteria (i.e., appearance) and general feather development patterns throughout the nestling period. On subsequent pages, averages and ranges of morphometric data and more-detailed descriptions of development are presented on a day-by-day basis.

Within the tables, we have attempted to list morphometric data in descending order of utility. Priority is given to characteristics with a fast growth rate, high ease and accuracy of measuring, and prominence in the literature. Priority was also given to those characteristics that proved useful for aging via field trials, preliminary analysis, and through prior experience aging altricial nestlings. For comparative purposes, the variables are listed in the same order for each day and species.

We recommend a systematic approach when using the tables for aging nestlings, beginning with an initial filtering of possible age ranges using the information on the first page of each species account. These age ranges can then be further refined through the use of the daily descriptions.

Measurements and Terminology

It is important that measurements are taken in a standard format, using terminology that is consistent. The variables described below were taken for each species in this guide and are presented in the account tables. For several of the measurements used, we followed guidelines as described by Pyle (1997) or Baldwin et al. (1931). Measurements taken with electronic calipers are to the nearest 0.01 mm and measurements taken with a ruler are to the nearest 0.5 mm. Weight was measured with an electronic scale to the nearest 0.1 g. A full treatment on the methods used to collect this data is provided in Appendix B.

Feather definitions:

Apteria: The naked spaces found between the feather tracts.

Contour feathers: The feathers of the head, body, and coverts excluding any remiges or rectrices.

Eruption: The breaking down of the pin sheath usually occurring at the distal tip of the pin, exposing the feather.

Neossoptiles: Down feathers present when a bird hatches.

Pterylae: Areas on the skin from which feathers grow; the feather tracts.

Papillae: A small projection of tissue usually used to describe feathers at an early stage of development prior to emergence from the skin.

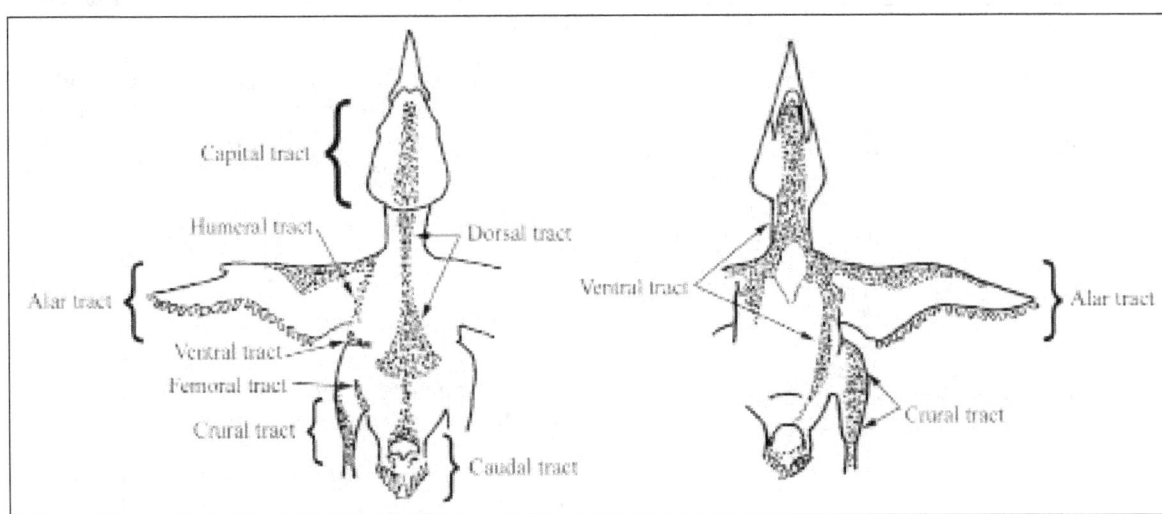

Fig. 1. Dorsal and ventral views of a nestling with the individual feather tracts marked and identified.

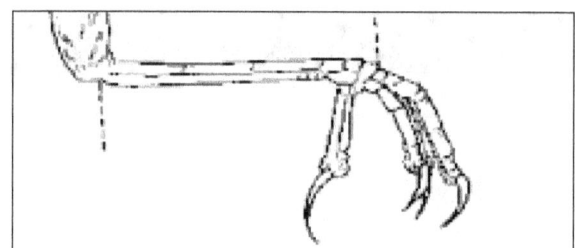

Fig. 2. Tarsus with measurement indicators at the tibiotarsus joint and distal end of the last leg scale.

Remiges: The flight feathers of the wing, including the primaries, secondaries, and tertials.

Rectrices: The flight feathers of the tail.

Teleoptiles: All flight and contour feathers found on a bird.

Weight. — Weight is taken by placing the bird directly on the scale (older chicks may need to be placed in a container). To reduce differences, this should be the last measurement taken so the nestling can defecate before weight is recorded.

Tarsus.—Tarsus is measured with calipers from the tibiotarsus joint to the distal end of the last leg scale before the toes emerge (Fig. 2). When it is difficult to see the end of the tibiotarsus joint, feel for it with fingertips; likewise, to find the last leg scale before the toes emerge, bend the foot and place one end of the calipers at the bend, checking that the bend is indeed at the distal end of the last leg scale. It may help to become familiar with the number of scales present on the ankle before the toes emerge. This helps because identifying the last leg scale can sometimes be difficult, especially in younger birds.

Wing chord.—Early in development, the wing is measured with a wing ruler from the bend of the wrist to tip of the distal segment of the forelimb. Once the primary pins have emerged, wing chord is measured with a wing ruler, unflattened, from the bend of the wrist to the tip of the primaries (Fig. 3).

Fig. 3. Wing chord as measured with a wing ruler; without flattening or pressing down on the wing.

Primary and rectrix pin lengths.—Pin lengths are measured with a ruler from the point of emergence from the skin to the end of the feather or pin (Fig. 4).

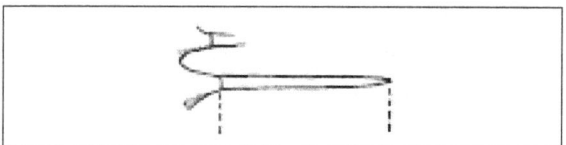

Fig. 4. Pin lengths as measured from the point of emergence from the skin.

Culmen.—Culmen is measured with calipers from the anterior end of the nostrils to the tip of the bill (Fig. 5). For practical reasons, the culmen in some species may need to be measured differently. Exposed culmen is an alternate measurement taken for some species and is measured along the ridge of the upper mandible from the tip of the feathers at the base of the bill to the bill tip. If you are uncertain about how to measure the bill in a species, you should consult the literature (Pyle 1997).

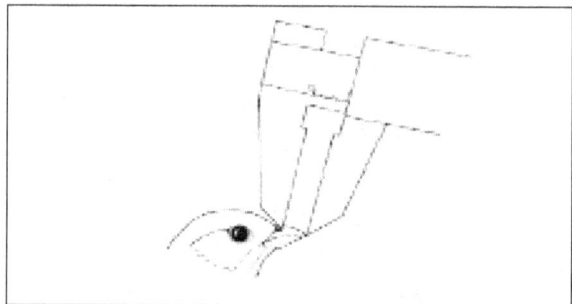

Fig. 5. The culmen as measured from nares to tip.

Eyes.—Eyes are described as closed, partially open when the eyelids begin to open, or fully open when they appear fully alert and exposed.

Total length.—Total length is a measure of body size and is taken from the tip of bill to the tip of the tail bud with the bird placed on its back along a ruler (Fig. 6). For consistency, the chick should be in a relaxed and natural position with its body and neck gently stretched out so that its bill is almost parallel with the ruler.

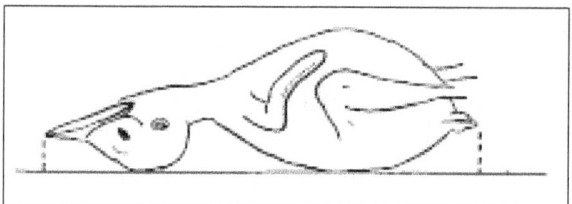

Fig. 6. Total length taken from the tip of the bill to the tail bud.

Longest broken primary.—The longest exposed primary (exposed feather portion only) is measured with a ruler from the point of emergence from the pin shaft to the distal tip of the feather itself (Fig. 7).

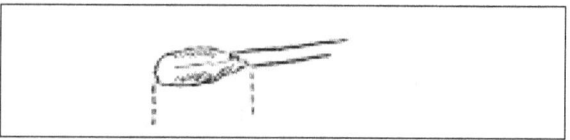

Fig. 7. The exposed portion of the longest broken primary as measured with a ruler.

Gape and rictus.—The gape (mouth opening) is measured with calipers at its widest length (Fig. 8). The pliable tissue (rictus) at base of the bill should not be bent or squeezed by the calipers during measurement of the gape. The gape can grow quickly early in the nestling period and measurements can increase or decrease greatly between days as the rictal tissue contracts and expands. Hence, the gape should be both measured and used with caution.

Fig. 8. The gape as measured with calipers.

Physical and behavioral descriptors.—Examples of behavioral data include movement and begging behavior, opening of eyes, call notes, shivering, and reaction to the observer. We describe appendage movement abilities and begging behavior as very slow and weak, periodic; slow and weak, but steady; quick and uncontrolled, frequent; or quick and deliberate. Any sounds, skin or bill color, and notable changes in appearance are also described.

Species Account Tables

Species information.—Species accounts start with nest-period information, important to aging nests found before hatching. Nest-period information includes means and ranges in clutch size, nest building time, incubation period, and nestling period. These parameters may vary temporally and spatially and are more accurate when calculated from your specific population (versus from the literature).

Indicator table.—This table provides an "at a glance" reference to prominent developmental events and their approximate day of appearance. Included are events that were found to be reliable for aging within one or two days and/or were easy to note visually. This table should be used together with the feather development table. The daily accounts can be consulted for more detail.

General feather development.—This table provides a quick reference to prominent feather development events and their approximate day of appearance. The general progression of feather development is shown to guide users to the approximate age range of nestlings. A range of possible ages should be selected using this table together with the indicator table described above. The daily accounts can then be consulted for more detail.

Key visual indicators.—List of visual descriptors we found to be prominent and reliable for each day that can serve to reinforce age estimates. Examples of descriptors include behavior, general appearance, color changes, etc. Typical dates for banding are noted here as are cautions regarding premature fledging ("jumping").

Photographs.—A representative photograph is presented for each day. These photos can be used by field biologists to become familiar with the general appearance of the nestlings, including the appearance of key visual indicators and feather tracts.

Feather tract data.—The percentage of individuals at a given developmental stage for each feather tract is presented. Feather development events are indicated respectively as "Not Visible - N", "Visible - V" (below skin), "Pin - P" (above and broken through skin), "Unsheathing - U" (feather partially exposed), or "Fully Unsheathed - F" for each individual tract (Fig. 9). The most advanced stage of a given feather tract is indicated. For example, a tract with exposed pins of which only a few are unsheathing is marked as U for unsheathing. Feather tracts are listed in the same order each day for ease of comparison across days. Tracts are listed beginning with the capital tract, then continuing posteriorly and ending with the ventral tract. The sample size in individuals is provided for each feather tract.

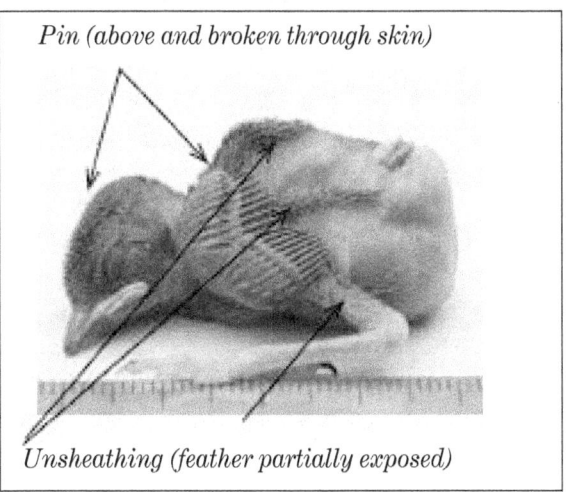

Fig. 9. Example of feather development and appearance, using a Wrentit on Day 7.

Morphometric data.—Growth data (mean, standard deviation, and range) are presented for several measurements to provide indices of body size for each day. The sample unit is the number of nestlings measured.

General description.—A more complete description of the appearance of feather tracts and behavioral characteristics is given for each day of nestling development.

Results

Dusky Flycatcher
Empidonax oberholseri
Data collection: Lassen National Forest, Tehama County, California. Nests: $n = 9$ (2004)
Nest Period Data: No data
Building: No data
Clutch size: No data
Incubation period: No data
Nestling period: No data

Indicator Table: Dusky Flycatcher visual characteristics typical at a given age.

Indicator characteristics	Age	Indicator characteristics	Age
No pins are visible	1	Dorsal and ventral tracts begin to unsheathe	7
Alar pins in a band centered across wing	2	All feather tracts begin to unsheathe	8
Alar pins have grown towards posterior edge of wing	3	Primary pins begin to unsheathe	9
Alar pins have grown to the wing edge and may be pushing out on skin	4	Young appear feathered due to extensive unsheathing	10
		Contrasting buffy wing bars are readily visible	10-11
Alar pins have emerged	4-5	Contour feather pins are not visible due to extensive unsheathing	12
Eyes begin to open	5-6		

General Feather Development: Dusky Flycatcher feather tract development by day. Most advanced stage is indicated as N-Not visible (not pigmented), V-Visible below skin, P-Pins above skin, U-Unsheathing, or F-Fully unsheathed.

Day	Capital	Dorsal	Humeral	Alar	Femoral	Crural	Caudal	Ventral
1	N	N	N	N V	N	N	N	N
2	N	N	N	N V	N	N	N	N V
3	N V	N V	N V	V	N V	N	N V	N V
4	V P	V P	V P	V P	V P	N V	V P	V P
5	V P	P	V P	V P	V P	V P	V P	V P
6	P	P U	P U	P	V P	V P	V P	P U
7	P	P U	P U	P U	P U	P U	P U	P U
8	U	U	U	U	U	U	U	U
9	U	U	U	U	U	U	U	U
10	U	U	U	U	U	U	U	U
11	U	U	U	U	U	U	U	U
12	U	U	U	U	U	U	U	U

Dusky Flycatcher *(Empidonax oberholseri)* continued

Day 1 Key Visual Indicators:

- No pins are visible
- Down may be matted
- Young are small (egg size)

Day 2 Key Visual Indicators:

- Subcutaneous alar pins just visible and centered along dorsal surface of wing

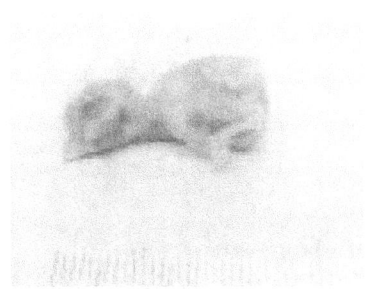

Feather Tract Development

Tract	N	V	P	U	F	n
Capital	100					12
Dorsal	100					12
Humeral	100					12
Alar	84	16				12
Femoral	100					12
Crural	100					12
Caudal	100					12
Ventral	100					12

Feather Tract Development

Tract	N	V	P	U	F	n
Capital	100					6
Dorsal	100					6
Humeral	100					6
Alar	33	67				6
Femoral	100					6
Crural	100					6
Caudal	100					6
Ventral	83	17				6

Morphometric Data

Measurements	Mean ± SD	Min	Max	n
Weight	1.475 ± 0.325	1.0	2.0	12
Tarsus	5.03 ± 0.486	4.5	5.8	12
Wing Chord	5.8 ± 0.411	5.3	6.5	12
Culmen	1.85 ± 0.392	1.4	2.5	12
Outer Primary	0	0	0	12
Outer Rectrix	0	0	0	12
Longest Broken Primary	0	0	0	12
Length	30.58 ± 2.392	28.0	35.0	12
Gape	6.74 ± 1.750	1.8	9.0	12

Morphometric Data

Measurements	Mean ± SD	Min	Max	n
Weight	1.95 ± 0.243	1.6	2.3	6
Tarsus	6.02 ± 0.585	5.5	7.1	6
Wing Chord	6.73 ± 0.787	5.8	7.8	6
Culmen	1.88 ± 0.214	1.5	2.1	6
Outer Primary	0	0	0	6
Outer Rectrix	0	0	0	6
Longest Broken Primary	0	0	0	6
Length	31.5 ± 1.643	28.0	35.0	6
Gape	7.2 ± 0.642	6.2	7.9	6

General Description

Eyes closed. Young are egg size. No pins are visible below skin. Down may be moist and matted down and is present on the capital, humeral, dorsal, alar, crural, and ventral tracts. Bill is orange-yellow.

General Description

Eyes closed. Alar pins are becoming visible, are individually distinguishable, and are centered along the dorsal surface of the wing. Ventral pins may just be visible. No other pins are visible.

Dusky Flycatcher *(Empidonax oberholseri)* continued

Day 3 Key Visual Indicators:

- Alar pins have grown towards posterior edge of wing
- All tracts may be visible except for crural tract
- No pins have emerged

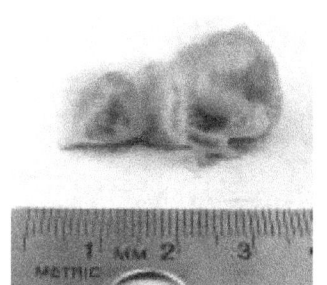

Feather Tract Development

Tract	N	V	P	U	F	*n*
Capital	33	67				12
Dorsal	8	92				12
Humeral	8	92				12
Alar		100				12
Femoral	33	67				12
Crural	100					12
Caudal	33	67				12
Ventral	17	83				12

Morphometric Data

Measurements	Mean ± SD	Min	Max	*n*
Weight	3.14 ± 0.626	2.1	4.1	12
Tarsus	6.28 ± 0.697	5.3	7.8	12
Wing Chord	7.46 ± 1.141	5.6	6.5	12
Culmen	2.21 ± 0.408	1.5	2.5	12
Outer Primary	0	0	0	12
Outer Rectrix	0	0	0	12
Longest Broken Primary	0	0	0	12
Length	35.75 ± 3.86	31.0	43.0	12
Gape	8.55 ± 0.843	6.6	9.5	12

General Description

Eyes closed. Capital tract may be visible as a few gray flecks. Dorsal tract visible as a light-gray stripe along the spine. Humeral tract visible as a short gray band. Alar pins have grown towards the posterior edge of wing. Femoral tract may appear as a few individual gray flecks. Crural tract is not visible. Caudal tract may appear as a thin light-gray band. Ventral tract is visible below skin.

Day 4 Key Visual Indicators:

- Alar pins have grown to the posterior edge of wing and may be pushing out on skin
- Young appear dark overall due to darkening and lengthening of subcutaneous pins

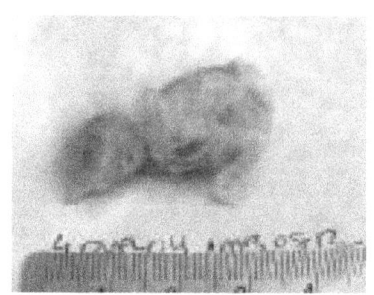

Feather Tract Development

Tract	N	V	P	U	F	*n*
Capital		62.5	37.5			8
Dorsal		62.5	37.5			8
Humeral		50	50			8
Alar		62.5	37.5			8
Femoral		88	12			8
Crural	37.5	62.5				8
Caudal		88	12			8
Ventral		50	50			8

Morphometric Data

Measurements	Mean ± SD	Min	Max	*n*
Weight	4.01 ± 0.574	3.2	5.0	10
Tarsus	8.59 ± 1.099	7.1	10.3	10
Wing Chord	9.55 ± 0.927	8.5	11.1	8
Culmen	2.49 ± 0.335	2.0	3.0	10
Outer Primary	0.1 ± 0.316	0	1.0	10
Outer Rectrix	0	0	0	10
Longest Broken Primary	0	0	0	10
Length	39.6 ± 3.098	35.0	44.0	10
Gape	9.24 ± 0.599	8.0	10.0	10

General Description

Eyes closed. Capital, dorsal, and humeral tracts have darkened and may be pressing up on skin surface. Alar pins have grown to the wing edge and may be pushing out on skin. Femoral pins have darkened and lengthened. Crural tract just becoming visible. Caudal tract is visible as a thin dark-gray band. Ventral pins may be pressing up on skin or some may be just emerging.

Dusky Flycatcher *(Empidonax oberholseri)* continued

Day 5 Key Visual Indicators:

- Alar pins have typically emerged
- Contour feather tracts beginning to emerge, just
  above skin surface

Day 6 Key Visual Indicators:

- Eyes typically opening
- All tracts have typically emerged
- Outer primary pins measure about 2mm in length

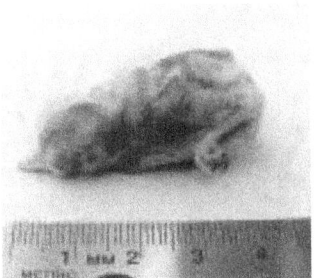

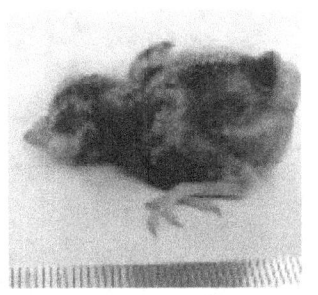

Feather Tract Development

Tract	N	V	P	U	F	n
Capital		25	75			8
Dorsal		12.5	87.5			8
Humeral		25	75			8
Alar		14	86			7
Femoral		25	75			8
Crural		37.5	62.5			8
Caudal		62.5	37.5			8
Ventral		12.5	87.5			8

Feather Tract Development

Tract	N	V	P	U	F	n
Capital			100			12
Dorsal			83	17		12
Humeral		25	75			8
Alar			100			12
Femoral		8	92			12
Crural		27	73			11
Caudal		27	73			11
Ventral			83	17		11

Morphometric Data

Measurements	Mean ± SD	Min	Max	n
Weight	4.91 ± 0.926	3.5	6.3	8
Tarsus	8.93 ± 0.991	7.4	10.1	8
Wing Chord	10.51 ± 3.064	3.8	13.4	8
Culmen	2.58 ± 0.324	2.1	3.2	8
Outer Primary	0.56 ± 0.678	0	2.0	8
Outer Rectrix	0	0	0	8
Longest Broken Primary	0	0	0	8
Length	43.25 ± 3.732	40.0	50.0	8
Gape	9.9 ± 0.321	9.5	10.6	8

Morphometric Data

Measurements	Mean ± SD	Min	Max	n
Weight	6.34 ± 0.981	4.4	8.3	12
Tarsus	11.03 ± 0.945	9.5	12.6	12
Wing Chord	13.15 ± 2.166	8.7	16.3	12
Culmen	2.83 ± 0.391	2.3	3.5	12
Outer Primary	2.13 ± 1.494	0.5	4.0	12
Outer Rectrix	0.13 ± 0.311	0	1.0	12
Longest Broken Primary	0	0	0	12
Length	43.83 ± 2.368	40.0	47.0	12
Gape	10.63 ± 0.502	9.9	11.5	12

General Description

Some individuals may begin to open their eyes. Bill is
becoming gray at the tip. Capital pins just beginning to
emerge. Dorsal and humeral tracts typically emerging.
Alar primary and secondary pins have emerged. Femoral
and crural tracts have lengthened and tips may be just
out. Caudal tract band has lengthened. Most ventral pins
have emerged.

General Description

Eyes typically beginning to open. Most capital tract pins
have emerged. Most dorsal pins have emerged and may
show light tips. Alar pins have emerged, including some
coverts. Primaries and secondaries may show light tips.
Several femoral and crural pins have emerged.

Dusky Flycatcher *(Empidonax oberholseri)* continued

Day 7 Key Visual Indicators:

- Dorsal and ventral tracts typically unsheathing
- Some alar tract coverts may be beginning to unsheathe

Day 8 Key Visual Indicators:

- All contour feather tracts typically unsheathing
- Some secondaries beginning to unsheathe

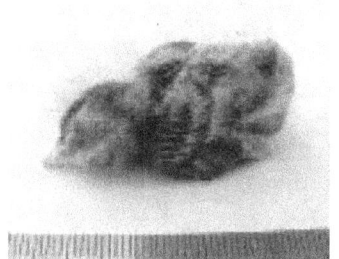

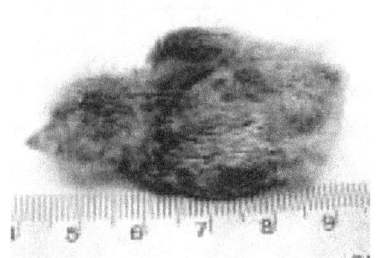

Feather Tract Development

Tract	N	V	P	U	F	n
Capital			100			3
Dorsal			33	67		3
Humeral			67	33		3
Alar			67	33		3
Femoral			67	33		3
Crural			67	33		3
Caudal			67	33		3
Ventral			33	67		3

Feather Tract Development

Tract	N	V	P	U	F	n
Capital				100		4
Dorsal				100		4
Humeral				100		4
Alar				100		4
Femoral				100		4
Crural				100		4
Caudal				100		4
Ventral				100		4

Morphometric Data

Measurements	Mean ± SD	Min	Max	n
Weight	8.33 ± 0.635	7.6	8.7	3
Tarsus	12.43 ± 1.00	11.4	13.4	3
Wing Chord	18.67 ± 1.963	16.4	19.8	3
Culmen	2.97 ± 0.115	2.9	3.1	3
Outer Primary	4.33 ± 0.577	4.0	5.0	3
Outer Rectrix	1.0 ± 0.0	1.0	1.0	3
Longest Broken Primary	0	0	0	3
Length	55.33 ± 2.887	50.0	55.0	3
Gape	11.4 ± 0.458	11.0	11.9	3

Morphometric Data

Measurements	Mean ± SD	Min	Max	n
Weight	8.81 ± 1.143	6.5	10.4	8
Tarsus	13.18 ± 1.051	11.6	14.5	8
Wing Chord	20.18 ± 4.713	10.1	24.0	8
Culmen	3.51 ± 0.372	3.2	4.3	8
Outer Primary	6.5 ± 2.074	4.0	9.0	6
Outer Rectrix	2.17 ± 1.169	1.0	4.0	6
Longest Broken Primary	0.38 ± 0.744	0	2.0	8
Length	51.0 ± 2.878	46.0	55.0	8
Gape	11.6 ± 0.875	10.1	12.8	8

General Description

Capital tract pins have lengthened and are still typically in pin. Dorsal pins have lengthened and some are beginning to unsheathe. All humeral pins have emerged and may begin to unsheathe. Alar pins have lengthened and coverts may be unsheathing. Some femoral and crural tracts may show white tips or have begun to unsheathe. Rectrices have begun to emerge. Ventral tract is typically unsheathing. Young grasp uncontrollably. Bill is becoming a purplish pink with a gray tip.

General Description

Capital tract pins have typically begun to unsheathe. Some secondaries are beginning to unsheathe. Primaries are showing white tips or just beginning to unsheathe. Most pins of all contour feathers have begun to unsheathe. Bill continues to darken and anteriorly gray. Young can move and grasp constantly.

Dusky Flycatcher *(Empidonax oberholseri)* continued

Day 9 Key Visual Indicators:

- Primary tips beginning to unsheathe

Day 10 Key Visual Indicators:

- Most alar pins have begun to unsheathe
- Young appear soft due to extent of unsheathing
- Young appear alert

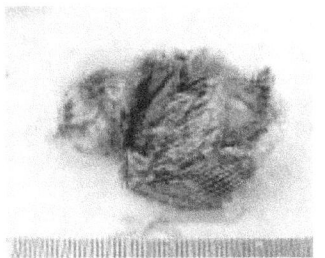

Feather Tract Development

Tract	N	V	P	U	F	n
Capital			25	75		8
Dorsal				100		8
Humeral				100		8
Alar				100		8
Femoral				100		8
Crural			25	75		8
Caudal			12.5	87.5		8
Ventral				100		8

Feather Tract Development

Tract	N	V	P	U	F	n
Capital				100		8
Dorsal				100		8
Humeral				100		7
Alar				100		8
Femoral				100		8
Crural				100		8
Caudal				100		8
Ventral				100		8

Morphometric Data

Measurements	Mean ± SD	Min	Max	n
Weight	9.075 ± 0.918	7.0	9.8	8
Tarsus	14.13 ± 1.412	11.4	16.2	8
Wing Chord	22.8 ± 2.370	19.8	25.8	8
Culmen	3.39 ± 0.426	2.6	3.9	8
Outer Primary	7.5 ± 2.204	4.0	10.0	8
Outer Rectrix	2.88 ± 1.246	1.0	5.0	8
Longest Broken Primary	0.88 ± 1.126	0	3.0	8
Length	53.38 ± 4.069	46.0	60.0	8
Gape	11.38 ± 0.373	11.1	12.0	8

Morphometric Data

Measurements	Mean ± SD	Min	Max	n
Weight	10.43 ± 1.132	8.3	11.9	8
Tarsus	14.69 ± 0.872	13.3	16.2	8
Wing Chord	28.95 ± 2.432	24.1	32.0	8
Culmen	3.89 ± 0.259	3.5	4.2	8
Outer Primary	12.5 ± 2.507	8.0	15.0	8
Outer Rectrix	5.13 ± 1.356	3.0	7.0	8
Longest Broken Primary	3.5 ± 1.927	1.0	6.0	8
Length	55.75 ± 3.770	50.0	61.0	8
Gape	11.7 ± 0.623	11.0	12.9	8

General Description

All feather tracts are clearly unsheathing, although sheaths may still be prominent on capital and dorsal tracts. Primary pins are beginning to unsheathe and most alar feathers are mostly in their sheath. Young are able to hop around, though are not well coordinated. May give contact "pip" calls.

General Description

All tracts continue to unsheathe and pin sheaths are mostly hidden by exposed feathers. Several primaries and secondaries are now unsheathed about 3-4 mm. Bill has turned about 75% gray. Young are alert and can hop.

Dusky Flycatcher *(Empidonax oberholseri)* continued

Day 11 Key Visual Indicators:

- Contrasting buffy wing bars are visible
- Young are very alert and can hop readily on the ground

Day 12 Key Visual Indicators:

- Contour feather pins are obscured due to extensive unsheathing
- May appear similar to Day 11

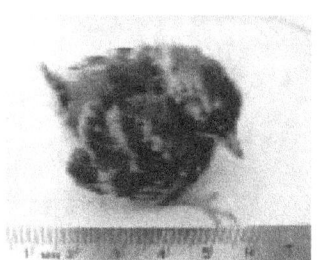

Feather Tract Development

Tract	N	V	P	U	F	n
Capital				100		6
Dorsal				100		6
Humeral				100		6
Alar				100		6
Femoral				100		6
Crural				100		6
Caudal				100		6
Ventral				100		6

Feather Tract Development

Tract	N	V	P	U	F	n
Capital				100		7
Dorsal				100		7
Humeral				100		7
Alar				100		7
Femoral				100		7
Crural				100		7
Caudal				100		7
Ventral				100		7

Morphometric Data

Measurements	Mean ± SD	Min	Max	n
Weight	10.3 ± 0.346	10.0	10.6	4
Tarsus	15.52 ± 1.134	13.5	16.5	6
Wing Chord	31.8 ± 3.295	27.8	35.5	6
Culmen	3.93 ± 0.398	3.4	4.4	6
Outer Primary	14.0 ± 3.033	9.0	17.0	6
Outer Rectrix	6.77 ± 2.002	3.0	9.0	6
Longest Broken Primary	6.67 ± 2.582	3.0	9.0	6
Length	55.5 ± 4.324	50.0	60.0	6
Gape	11.97 ± 0.294	11.6	12.4	6

Morphometric Data

Measurements	Mean ± SD	Min	Max	n
Weight	11.22 ± 1.030	9.2	12.1	6
Tarsus	16.03 ± 0.325	15.5	16.4	7
Wing Chord	37.8 ± 2.204	34.1	40.5	7
Culmen	4.24 ± 0.416	3.5	4.8	7
Outer Primary	17.57 ± 1.134	16.0	19.0	7
Outer Rectrix	11.0 ± 1.155	9.0	12.0	7
Longest Broken Primary	11.0 ± 6.880	1.0	17.0	7
Length	62.29 ± 2.360	59.0	66.0	7
Gape	12.2 ± 0.455	11.7	13.1	7

General Description

All feather tracts continue to unsheathe extensively. Primaries are unsheathed about 6-7mm. Contrasting buffy wing bars are clearly visible along the wing coverts. Bill has darkened almost entirely except for the gape. Nestlings are prone to "jump" on this day. Use caution.

General Description

Nestlings appear very similar to Day 11. Wing chord and longest broken primary have substantially increased in length. Contour feather pins are obscured by unsheathed feathers. Nestlings should not be handled if they appear prone to jump from the nest.

Carolina Wren
Thryothorus ludovicianus ludovicianus
Data collection location: Tennessee Valley Authority Reservation, Muscle Shoals, Colbert County, Alabama
Nests: $n = 3$ (2001), $n = 2$ (2002), $n = 16$ (2004)
Nest Period Data (Haggerty and Morton 1995): Average (range), n = number of nests
Building: no data
Clutch size: 4.3 (3 – 6) eggs, $n = 88$
Incubation: 14.8 (12 - 16) days, $n = 16$
Nestling: 12.2 (10 - 16) days, $n = 5$

Indicator Table: Carolina Wren visual characteristics typical at a given age.

Indicator characteristics	Age	Indicator characteristics	Age
Alar pins in a band centered across wing	1	Alar pin tips appear pale, ready to unsheathe	6
Down is matted or moist	1	Alar pins begin to unsheathe	7
Alar pins stretched towards posterior edge	2	Pins of most tracts appear ready to unsheathe	7
Primaries and secondaries just emerged	3	Contour tracts except capital begin to unsheathe	8
Pins of humeral, dorsal, and capital tracts appear ready to emerge	4	All feather tracts clearly unsheathing	9
Eyes begin to open	4-5		

General Feather Development: Carolina Wren feather tract development by day. Most advanced stage is indicated as N-Not visible (not pigmented), V-Visible below skin, P-Pins above skin, U-Unsheathing, or F-Fully unsheathed.

Day	Capital	Dorsal	Humeral	Alar	Femoral	Crural	Caudal	Ventral
1	N	N	N V	V	N	N	N	N
2	N V	N V	N V	V P	N	N	N V	N V
3	N V	N V	N V	V P	N V	N V	N V	N V
4	V	V	V P	P	N V	N V	N V	N V
5	V P	V P	V P	P	V P	V P	V P	V P
6	V P	V P	V P	P U	V P	V P	V P	V P U
7	V P U	P U	P U	P U	P U	P U	P U	P U
8	P U	P U	P U	U	P U	P U	P U	U
9	P U	U	U	U	U	U	U	U
10	U	U	U	U	U	U	U	U

Day 1 Key Visual Indicators:

- Subcutaneous alar pins are centered along the dorsal wing surface
- Most other feather tracts are not visible below skin
- Down is often matted and moist, young are egg size.

Day 2 Key Visual Indicators:

- Alar pins stretched to posterior edge of wing

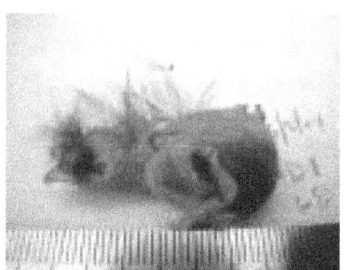

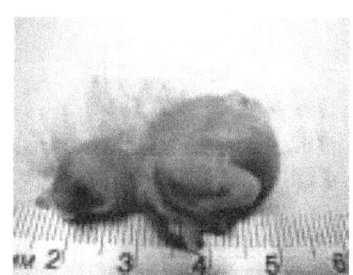

Feather Tract Development

Tract	N	V	P	U	F	n
Capital	100					35
Dorsal	100					36
Humeral	97	3				36
Alar		100				36
Femoral	100					36
Crural	100					35
Caudal	100					36
Ventral	100					36

Feather Tract Development

Tract	N	V	P	U	F	n
Capital	88	12				26
Dorsal	52	48				27
Humeral	52	48				27
Alar		70	30			27
Femoral	100					27
Crural	100					26
Caudal	93	7				27
Ventral	96	4				27

Morphometric Data

Measurements	Mean ± SD	Min	Max	n
Weight	2.24 ± 0.398	1.6	3.25	36
Tarsus	6.69 ± 0.475	5.6	7.9	36
Wing Chord	6.29 ± 0.541	4.4	7.6	36
Culmen	2.05 ± 0.210	1.6	2.4	36
Outer Primary	0	0	0	26
Outer Rectrix	0	0	0	34
Longest Broken Primary	0	0	0	26
Length	35.5 ± 2.302	32.0	40.0	26
Gape	8.34 ± 0.696	7.1	9.8	24

Morphometric Data

Measurements	Mean ± SD	Min	Max	n
Weight	3.13 ± 0.417	2.4	4.0	27
Tarsus	7.67 ± 0.444	6.6	8.7	27
Wing Chord	7.12 ± 0.459	6.4	8.4	27
Culmen	2.35 ± 0.197	2.0	2.8	27
Outer Primary	0	0	0	21
Outer Rectrix	0	0	0	26
Longest Broken Primary	0	0	0	21
Length	39.5 ± 2.524	36.0	45.0	20
Gape	9.51 ± 0.485	8.6	10.2	19

General Description

Eyes closed and lids appear dark. Bill pale, except for dark tip; rictus cream yellow to spectrum yellow at corners. Skin is reddish-pink. Grayish-brown down on capital, humeral and spinal tracts; often matted. Distinct, dark primary and secondary pin feathers visible below skin in alar tract; pins still very small and centered across dorsal surface of wings. No pigmented pins usually visible below skin in other tracts. Moves limbs and head very slowly. Soft "pep" calls heard. Often remains in curled, embryo-like position with head resting on large protruding abdomen.

General Description

Eyes closed. Humeral and dorsal tracts may have very small, dark pigmented pins below skin; appear as small dark dots. Alar pins under skin larger and merge to give arm, especially hand, a dark color; no flesh-colored stripe visible along posterior edge of dorsal surface of arm. Pigmented pins usually not visible under skin in other tracts. Skin more flesh colored, less reddish than day 1. Down fluffy, not matted. Slowly lifts head and begs; often remains in curled up position.

Carolina Wren *(Thryothorus ludovicianus ludovicianus)* continued

Day 3 Key Visual Indicators:

- Primaries and some secondaries emerged
- Longest primary usually <1mm

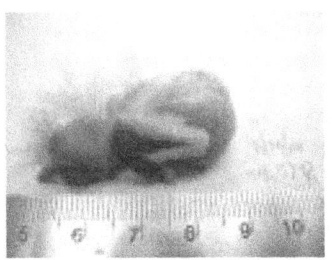

Day 4 Key Visual Indicators:

- Pins of humeral, dorsal, and capital tracts appear ready to emerge
- Longest primary usually between 1 - 2mm
- Pigmented pins becoming visible on ventral tract near chest and axilla

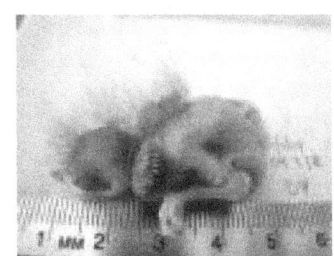

Feather Tract Development

Tract	N	V	P	U	F	n
Capital	6	97				33
Dorsal	6	94				33
Humeral	3	97				33
Alar		6	97			33
Femoral	76	24				33
Crural	30	70				33
Caudal	21	79				33
Ventral	55	45				33

Feather Tract Development

Tract	N	V	P	U	F	n
Capital		100				24
Dorsal		100				25
Humeral		96	4			25
Alar			100			25
Femoral	32	68				25
Crural	8	92				24
Caudal	4	96				25
Ventral	24	76				25

Morphometric Data

Measurements	Mean ± SD	Min	Max	n
Weight	4.70 ± 0.806	3.3	6.7	33
Tarsus	9.16 ± 0.764	7.9	11.0	33
Wing Chord	8.95 ± 0.847	7.8	12.0	33
Culmen	2.66 ± 0.212	2.3	3.0	33
Outer Primary	0.60 ± 0.400	0	2.0	26
Outer Rectrix	0	0	0	31
Longest Broken Primary	0	0	0	27
Length	44.04 ± 3.130	36.0	50.0	26
Gape	10.46 ± 0.638	9.5	12.1	25

Morphometric Data

Measurements	Mean ± SD	Min	Max	n
Weight	6.20 ± 1.119	4.2	9.5	25
Tarsus	10.82 ± 1.063	9.0	13.9	25
Wing Chord	11.32 ± 1.386	8.7	15.8	25
Culmen	3.15 ± 0.257	2.7	3.5	25
Outer Primary	1.84 ± 0.846	1.0	4.0	23
Outer Rectrix	0.02 ± 0.10	0	0.5	25
Longest Broken Primary	0	0	0	23
Length	49.70 ± 3.560	42.0	58.0	23
Gape	11.67 ± 0.658	10.5	13.0	23

General Description

Eyes closed. Pins of alar tract clearly emerged. Pale tissue bands may be present in ventral tract and femoral tract. Subcutaneous pigmented pins in femoral tract may be visible as small flecks. Dark subcutaneous pins clearly visible in spinal, humeral and capital tracts. Longest primary pin (P7) usually 1 mm or less. Caudal tract visible as subcutaneous gray color and emerged hair-like pin tips may be visible. Crural tract may have very small pigmented subcutaneous pins. Upper bill brownish. Movements more frequent and strong.

General Description

Eyes partially opened. Longest primary measures between 1 and 2 mm. Dark, subcutaneous pins visible in chest area of ventral tract. Dark subcutaneous pins in capital, femoral, caudal and crural tracts. Subcutaneous pins of spinal and humeral tracts appear ready to emerge through skin. Can move body with kicks and wing flaps.

Carolina Wren *(Thryothorus ludovicianus ludovicianus)* continued

Day 5 Key Visual Indicators:

- Pins on most tracts just emerged or appear ready to emerge
- All alar pins including coverts have emerged
- Eyes typically appear partially to fully open

Day 6 Key Visual Indicators:

- Pins on all tracts have emerged
- Tips of primary pins are pale, appear ready to unsheathe

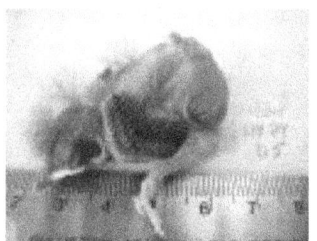

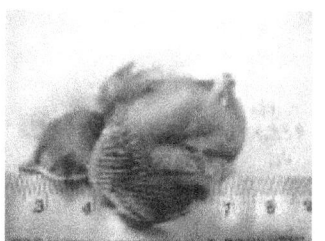

Feather Tract Development

Tract	N	V	P	U	F	n
Capital		88	12			33
Dorsal		60	40			33
Humeral		55	45			33
Alar			100			33
Femoral		79	18	3		33
Crural		67	33			33
Caudal		70	30			33
Ventral		79	21			33

Feather Tract Development

Tract	N	V	P	U	F	n
Capital		33	67			24
Dorsal		16	84			25
Humeral		8	92			25
Alar			92	8		25
Femoral		24	76			25
Crural		29	71			24
Caudal		16	84			25
Ventral		20	72	8		25

Morphometric Data

Measurements	Mean ± SD	Min	Max	n
Weight	8.20 ± 1.158	5.9	11.1	33
Tarsus	13.03 ± 0.967	11.4	16.2	33
Wing Chord	15.25 ± 1.860	11.2	20.5	33
Culmen	3.67 ± 0.347	3.0	4.4	33
Outer Primary	4.14 ± 1.757	0	9.0	26
Outer Rectrix	0.10 ± 0.201	0	0.5	31
Longest Broken Primary	0.02 ± 0.096	0	0.5	27
Length	53.19 ± 4.350	43.0	65.0	27
Gape	12.36 ± 0.646	11.2	14.4	25

Morphometric Data

Measurements	Mean ± SD	Min	Max	n
Weight	9.98 ± 1.484	6.4	13.1	25
Tarsus	15.11 ± 1.021	13.0	18.0	25
Wing Chord	19.18 ± 2.483	14.7	25.6	25
Culmen	4.08 ± 0.437	3.1	4.9	25
Outer Primary	7.64 ± 2.097	4.5	13.0	22
Outer Rectrix	0.33 ± 0.396	0	1.2	24
Longest Broken Primary	0.05 ± 0.147	0	0.5	22
Length	58.13 ± 4.703	47.0	66.0	23
Gape	12.66 ± 0.516	11.6	13.7	23

General Description

Eyes open. Ventral, dorsal, femoral, humeral, crural and caudal tracts have emerged pins or pins that appear ready to emerge. Capital pins may emerge in nape region. Bill and skin of face dark, contrasts with yellow rictus. Can move body with kicks and wing flaps.

General Description

Eyes open. Pins usually emerged in all tracts. Begs directly at nest entrance. May cower and snap bill (inaudible) when nest is disturbed. Kicks and flaps quickly and can easily turn itself over when placed on back. Tips of alar pins pale and look ready to unsheathe. Face dark and contrasts sharply with yellow rictus.

Carolina Wren (*Thryothorus ludovicianus ludovicianus*) continued

Day 7 Key Visual Indicators:

- Alar pins beginning to unsheathe
- Pins of most tracts have pale tips and appear ready to unsheathe

Day 8 Key Visual Indicators:

- All feather tracts typically unsheathing except capital and caudal
- Appears alert and active

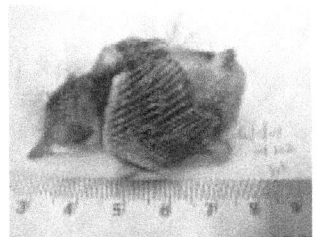

Feather Tract Development

Tract	N	V	P	U	F	n
Capital		3	94	3		29
Dorsal			80	20		30
Humeral			83	17		30
Alar			50	50		30
Femoral			77	23		30
Crural			90	10		29
Caudal			90	10		30
Ventral			70	30		30

Feather Tract Development

Tract	N	V	P	U	F	n
Capital			78	22		23
Dorsal			21	79		24
Humeral			21	79		24
Alar				100		24
Femoral			4	96		24
Crural			48	52		23
Caudal			71	29		24
Ventral				100		24

Morphometric Data

Measurements	Mean ± SD	Min	Max	n
Weight	11.90 ± 1.557	7.3	14.9	30
Tarsus	17.07 ± 0.974	13.9	18.6	30
Wing Chord	24.04 ± 2.440	17.5	28.4	30
Culmen	4.46 ± 0.369	3.6	5.2	30
Outer Primary	11.53 ± 2.337	8.0	17.0	20
Outer Rectrix	1.15 ± 0.847	0	4.0	28
Longest Broken Primary	0.38 ± 0.705	0	3.0	20
Length	63.45 ± 4.751	55.0	73.0	20
Gape	12.84 ± 0.661	11.8	14.6	20

Morphometric Data

Measurements	Mean ± SD	Min	Max	n
Weight	13.53 ± 1.726	8.4	16.15	24
Tarsus	18.55 ± 1.062	16.0	20.7	24
Wing Chord	28.18 ± 2.645	19.6	33.2	24
Culmen	4.92 ± 0.395	4.2	5.9	24
Outer Primary	14.17 ± 4.222	1.3	21.0	20
Outer Rectrix	2.23 ± 1.280	0	6.0	23
Longest Broken Primary	2.08 ± 1.315	0.5	6.0	19
Length	66.80 ± 6.978	53.0	80.0	20
Gape	13.03 ± 0.608	12.0	14.0	20

General Description

Alar pin tips pale and often unsheathing. Ventral, dorsal, humeral, and femoral tracts have pins that look ready to open and unsheathing may begin. Can hold head up off clipboard. Pins of ventral and femoral tracts cinnamon colored.

General Description

All tracts but capital and caudal have pins that are clearly ruptured. Very alert; flaps and kicks vigorously, and usually will not remain still during handling. Eyes typically stay open during handling. Eyes and face black. May give fledgling "chip" locator call. Young are typically ready for banding.

Day 9 Key Visual Indicators:

- All feather tracts clearly unsheathed
- Light brown feathers of ventral tract form two
  broad stripes
- Rust colored dorsal feathers form strip on back

Feather Tract Development

Tract	N	V	P	U	F	*n*
Capital			9	91		22
Dorsal				100		23
Humeral				100		23
Alar				100		23
Femoral				100		23
Crural			5	95		22
Caudal			4	96		23
Ventral				100		23

Morphometric Data

Measurements	Mean ± SD	Min	Max	*n*
Weight	14.85 ± 1.437	10.4	16.5	23
Tarsus	19.77 ± 0.888	18.0	21.5	23
Wing Chord	32.93 ± 1.779	28.5	36.4	23
Culmen	5.16 ± 0.455	4.2	6.0	23
Outer Primary	19.35 ± 2.731	14.0	22.2	15
Outer Rectrix	3.85 ± 0.918	2.0	6.0	21
Longest Broken Primary	5.27 ± 1.280	3.0	8.0	15
Length	71.53 ± 5.805	60.0	83.0	15
Gape	12.75 ± 0.507	12.0	13.5	15

General Description

All tracts have pins that are clearly unsheathed. Upper
wing covert pins clearly unsheathed. Unsheathed feathers
of ventral tract cinnamon colored and form two broad
strips. Unsheathed feathers of dorsal tract form rust
colored strip on back. Very alert; flaps and kicks quickly,
and nestling usually will not remain still. Turns neck and
head to look around. May give fledgling "chip" locator call.
Young are prone to "jump" after this day. Use caution.

Wrentit

Chamea fasciata rufula
Data collection: Point Reyes National Seashore, Marin Co., California.   Nests: $n = 2$ (2003), $n = 2$ (2004), $n = 7$ (2005)
Nest Period Data: Average (range), n = number of nests
Building: 6-7 (3 - 14) days (Geupel and Ballard, 2002)
Clutch size: 3.6 (1 - 5) eggs, $n = 733$
Incubation: 14.9 (11 - 18) days, $n = 192$
Nestling: 14.6 (11 - 19) days, $n = 242$

Indicator Table: Wrentit visual characteristics typical at a given age.

Indicator characteristics	Age	Indicator characteristics	Age
Alar pins centered on dorsal wing surface	1	Capital, dorsal, and humeral tracts just emerged	6
Alar pins stretched towards posterior edge of wing	2	Eyes begin to open	6-7
Crural tract just becoming visible	3	Alar pin tips are pale, ready to unsheathe	8
Alar pins have extended to the wing edge	3	Alar pins begin to unsheathe	9
Primary and secondary pins appear ready to emerge	4	Young appear soft due to extent of unsheathing	10

General Feather Development: Wrentit feather tract development by day. Most advanced stage is indicated as N-Not visible (not pigmented), V-Visible below skin, P-Pins above skin, U-Unsheathing, or F-Fully unsheathed.

Day	Capital	Dorsal	Humeral	Alar	Femoral	Crural	Caudal	Ventral
1	N	V	N V	V	N V	N	N V	N
2	N V	V	V	V	V	N	N V	N V
3	V	V	V	V	V	N V	V	V
4	V	V	V	V P	V	V	V	V
5	V	V P	V P	V P	V	V	V	V P
6	V P	V P U	V P U	P	V P U	V	V P	V P U
7	P	P U	P U	P U	V P U	V P U	V P U	P U
8	U	U	U	P U	U	V P U	P U	P U
9	U	U	U	U	U	P U	U	U
10	U	U	U	U	U	U	U	U
11	U	U	U	U	U	U	U	U

Wrentit *(Chamea fasciata rufula)* continued

Day 1 Key Visual Indicators:

- Skin appears uniformly fleshy pink except around eyes
- Capital tract pins are not visible
- Alar pins are centered along dorsal wing surface

Feather Tract Development

Tract	N	V	P	U	F	n
Capital	100					6
Dorsal		100				6
Humeral	50	50				6
Alar		100				6
Femoral	83	17				6
Crural	100					6
Caudal	50	50				6
Ventral	100					6

Morphometric Data

Measurements	Mean ± SD	Min	Max	n
Weight	1.78 ± 0.248	1.6	2.1	6
Tarsus	6.27 ± 1.310	4.58	7.2	6
Wing Chord	4.31 ± 0.696	3.5	5.17	6
Culmen	1.93 ± 0.305	1.6	2.27	4
Outer Primary	0	0	0	6
Outer Rectrix	0	0	0	6
Longest Broken Primary	0	0	0	5
Length	32.5 ± 1.291	31.0	34.0	4
Gape	7.32 ± 0.282	7.08	7.7	4

General Description

Eyes and ears closed. Ears visible as indentations. Bill is ocher with orange yellow, with an ashy olive tip, and a sulfur yellow gape. The nares are just barely visible. A very small white egg tooth is visible. Skin color is uniformly fleshy pink throughout head and body except for around the eyes, which are blackish gray. Head and body are completely naked. Capital, dorsal, humeral, and caudal tracts are visible as very light gray areas formed by faintly pigmented pins. Femoral and ventral tracts not visible. Flight feather pins on the wings are distinguishable as individual pins and are centered on the wing as a gray band. Limbs are moved around slowly. Young are struggling to lift head up.

Day 2 Key Visual Indicators:

- Back of head beginning to darken as capital tract pins begin to darken
- Dorsal tract area beginning to darken forming a light gray stripe
- Alar pins stretched towards posterior edge of wing

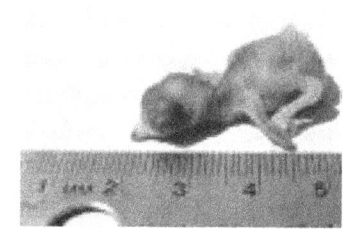

Feather Tract Development

Tract	N	V	P	U	F	n
Capital	27	73				11
Dorsal		100				11
Humeral		100				11
Alar		100				11
Femoral		100				11
Crural	100					11
Caudal	18	82				11
Ventral	55	45				11

Morphometric Data

Measurements	Mean ± SD	Min	Max	n
Weight	2.43 ± 0.548	1.7	3.4	9
Tarsus	7.69 ± 1.024	6.02	9.13	11
Wing Chord	5.0 ± 0.597	4.0	6.03	11
Culmen	2.22 ± 0.277	1.93	2.67	9
Outer Primary	0	0	0	11
Outer Rectrix	0	0	0	11
Longest Broken Primary	0	0	0	11
Length	33.8 ± 2.348	29.0	36.0	10
Gape	8.02 ± 0.605	6.87	8.94	10

General Description

Eyes and ears closed. Nares visible as a short notch. Egg tooth may still be present, though not as prominent as day 1. Skin is fleshy pink except for the area around eyes, top of head, and dorsal tract areas, which are blackish gray and wrinkled. Capital tract pins visible as light spots. Femoral tract is just visible as spotting. Dorsal tract is visible as a blackish gray stripe (1-2 mm wide). Ventral tract visible as gray spotting down the throat and sides of chest, becoming flesh colored along belly. Alar pins are individually distinguishable and are stretched towards the posterior edge of the wing. Humeral tract is visible as spotting forming a light gray band. Crural tract is not visible. Caudal tract is just visible. Young are able to move limbs quickly; are uncoordinated.

Wrentit *(Chamea fasciata rufula)* continued

Day 3 Key Visual Indicators:

- Alar pins have grown to the posterior edge of wing and press up on dorsal wing surface
- Crural tract just becoming visible as gray flecks

Day 4 Key Visual Indicators:

- Primary and secondary pins appear ready to emerge

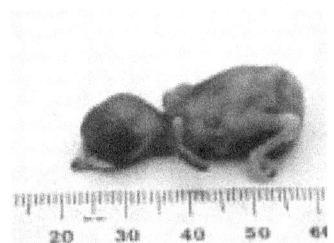

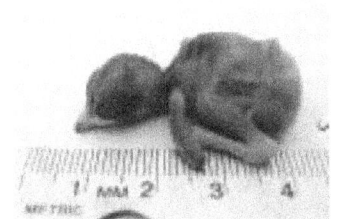

Feather Tract Development

Tract	N	V	P	U	F	n
Capital		100				13
Dorsal		100				13
Humeral		100				13
Alar		100				13
Femoral		100				13
Crural	38	62				13
Caudal		100				13
Ventral		100				13

Feather Tract Development

Tract	N	V	P	U	F	n
Capital		100				12
Dorsal		100				12
Humeral		100				12
Alar		92	8			12
Femoral		100				12
Crural		100				12
Caudal		100				12
Ventral		100				12

Morphometric Data

Measurements	Mean ± SD	Min	Max	n
Weight	3.51 ± 0.668	2.4	4.5	13
Tarsus	9.17 ± 0.937	7.64	10.73	13
Wing Chord	5.54 ± 0.520	5.0	6.51	13
Culmen	2.52 ± 0.229	2.16	2.88	12
Outer Primary	0	0	0	13
Outer Rectrix	0	0	0	13
Longest Broken Primary	0	0	0	12
Length	38.08 ± 2.275	34.0	42.0	12
Gape	9.16 ± 0.688	8.25	9.94	12

Morphometric Data

Measurements	Mean ± SD	Min	Max	n
Weight	4.42 ± 0.804	3.4	6.2	12
Tarsus	10.60 ± 1.406	8.01	13.02	12
Wing Chord	6.96 ± 1.573	5.5	10.0	12
Culmen	2.55 ± 0.230	2.05	2.8	12
Outer Primary	0.08 ± 0.289	0	1.0	12
Outer Rectrix	0	0	0	12
Longest Broken Primary	0	0	0	12
Length	42.0 ± 2.697	39.0	47.0	12
Gape	9.80 ± 0.824	8.61	11.1	12

General Description

Eyes closed. Ears closed. Remnant of egg tooth still may be visible. Skin a darker more purple fleshy pink. Skin around head is dark gray with much wrinkling. Capital tract is visible as gray flecks. Humeral tract is visible as a dark stripe about 5 mm in length. Dorsal tract is visible as a dark gray stripe with a separate darkened area near base of tail bud. Alar pins have extended to the edge of the wing and are pressing up on the dorsal surface of the wing. Femoral tract is visible as dark gray flecks in 2-3 short rows. Crural tract is just visible as a few gray flecks. Ventral tract is visible as gray flecks down the throat and sides of chest.

General Description

Eyes and ears closed. Nestlings are mostly naked. Capital tract is visible as flecks covering the head. Humeral and femoral tracts are visible as short dark gray stripes. Primary and secondary pins appear ready to emerge. Some body pins are pressing out against skin. Dorsal tract appears as a solid dark gray wrinkled stripe. Crural tract is visible as gray flecks. Individual caudal pins are distinguishable. Small hair-like projections appear where the rectrices will protrude. Ventral tract appears as a darker, more pronounced stripe composed of gray pins anteriorly and flesh colored pins posteriorly. Young sporadically lift body and head by kicking with their legs and flapping wings.

Wrentit *(Chamea fasciata rufula)* continued

Day 5 Key Visual Indicators:

- Capital, dorsal, humeral, and femoral tracts pushing up on skin surface, appear ready to emerge
- Alar pins typically just emerged

Day 6 Key Visual Indicators:

- Capital, dorsal, and humeral tracts just emerged
- Eyes typically begin to open
- Outer primary measures 1-2mm

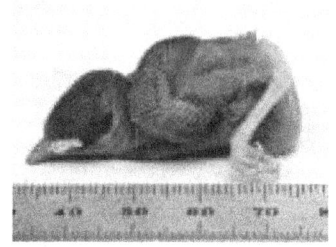

Feather Tract Development

Tract	N	V	P	U	F	n
Capital		100				10
Dorsal		90	10			10
Humeral		80	20			10
Alar		40	60			10
Femoral		100				10
Crural		100				10
Caudal		100				10
Ventral		90	10			10

Feather Tract Development

Tract	N	V	P	U	F	n
Capital		43	57			14
Dorsal		14	64	22		14
Humeral		14	72	14		14
Alar			100			14
Femoral		50	36	14		14
Crural		100				14
Caudal		71	29			14
Ventral		29	57	14		14

Morphometric Data

Measurements	Mean ± SD	Min	Max	n
Weight	5.61 ± 0.522	5.1	6.9	10
Tarsus	12.41 ± 1.664	9.56	15.15	10
Wing Chord	9.7 ± 2.275	6.0	13.0	10
Culmen	3.06 ± 0.162	2.84	3.3	8
Outer Primary	0.35 ± 0.242	0	0.5	10
Outer Rectrix	0	0	0	9
Longest Broken Primary	0	0	0	8
Length	43.75 ± 2.550	40.0	46.0	8
Gape	10.60 ± 0.362	10.17	11.03	8

Morphometric Data

Measurements	Mean ± SD	Min	Max	n
Weight	6.96 ± 0.592	5.7	8.0	14
Tarsus	14.44 ± 1.715	11.66	17.79	14
Wing Chord	12.61 ± 3.420	6.0	19.5	14
Culmen	3.13 ± 0.268	2.53	3.53	12
Outer Primary	1.35 ± 0.798	0	30.0	13
Outer Rectrix	0	0	0	13
Longest Broken Primary	0	0	0	12
Length	47.27 ± 2.149	45.0	51.0	11
Gape	10.98 ± 0.484	10.24	11.99	12

General Description

Eyes closed. Ear canals may begin to open. Nestlings are mostly naked with most feather tract pins now pushing up on the skin surface. Dark bill tip color now extends to all other parts of the bill except for the rictus and nares. The rictus is turning a deeper yellow and the area around the nares is an olive buff yellow. Capital tract pins have begun to push up on the skin. Anterior humeral pins and some ventral pins may have just emerged. Some or all primaries and secondaries typically emerging.

General Description

Eyes may begin to partially open. Ear canals appear open. Nestlings appear "spiky", with many pins now just out above the skin surface. The area around the nares is turning ash olive in color. Most primary and secondary pins have emerged. 9th primary measures 1-2 mm. Some wing covert pins may have emerged. Ventral pins may be just out with the exception of those anterior to the furculum. Crural tract pins have not emerged. Caudal tract typically not emerged.

Wrentit *(Chamea fasciata rufula)* continued

Day 7 Key Visual Indicators:

- Dorsal, humeral, femoral, and ventral tracts begin to unsheathe
- Caudal pins have emerged
- Eyes typically partially open

Day 8 Key Visual Indicators:

- Most feather tracts typically just unsheathing except for crural and caudal tract

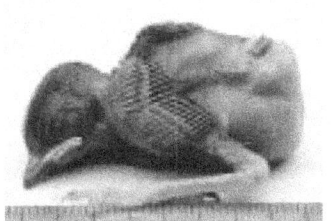

Feather Tract Development

Tract	N	V	P	U	F	n
Capital			85	15		13
Dorsal			69	31		13
Humeral			38	62		13
Alar			85	15		13
Femoral		8	38	54		13
Crural		70	15	15		13
Caudal		15	77	8		13
Ventral			38	62		13

Feather Tract Development

Tract	N	V	P	U	F	n
Capital			37.5	62.5		8
Dorsal				100		8
Humeral				100		8
Alar			12.5	87.5		8
Femoral				100		8
Crural			75	25		8
Caudal			62.5	37.5		8
Ventral			12.5	87.5		8

Morphometric Data

Measurements	Mean ± SD	Min	Max	n
Weight	7.74 ± 0.900	6.8	10.0	14
Tarsus	16.16 ± 1.430	14.15	18.7	14
Wing Chord	14.76 ± 2.793	9.0	20.0	14
Culmen	3.44 ± 0.195	3.17	3.79	12
Outer Primary	2.75 ± 1.141	1.0	5.0	14
Outer Rectrix	0.32 ± 0.249	0	0.5	14
Longest Broken Primary	0.04 ± 0.144	0	0.5	12
Length	48.42 ± 2.999	44.0	54.0	12
Gape	11.15 ± 0.513	10.23	12.23	12

Morphometric Data

Measurements	Mean ± SD	Min	Max	n
Weight	8.75 ± 0.327	8.4	9.2	6
Tarsus	17.25 ± 1.032	15.31	18.38	8
Wing Chord	18.2 ± 1.010	17.0	20.0	8
Culmen	3.68 ± 0.200	3.38	3.97	6
Outer Primary	4.29 ± 0.907	3.0	5.18	8
Outer Rectrix	0.63 ± 0.231	0.5	1.0	8
Longest Broken Primary	0	0	0	6
Length	50.67 ± 1.033	49.0	52.0	6
Gape	11.2 ± 0.451	10.61	11.81	6

General Description

Eyes are partially open. Bill continues to darken. Dorsal, humeral, femoral, and ventral tracts begin to unsheathe. Most pins of the remiges have clearly emerged. P9 measures about 5 mm.

General Description

Eyes are partially open. Bill continues to darken. All tracts except crural and caudal are now typically beginning to unsheathe. Remiges have lengthened, and their tips may appear white and ready to unsheathe. P9 measures about 7 mm. Some wing coverts and secondaries may be unsheathing. Movement is constant but uncoordinated.

Wrentit *(Chamea fasciata rufula)* continued

Day 9 Key Visual Indicators:

- Primary tips appear pale and ready to unsheathe or begin to unsheathe
- All feather tracts are unsheathing
- Secondary pins begin to unsheathe

Day 10 Key Visual Indicators:

- Capital, dorsal, and ventral tracts appear feathered due to the extent of exposed feathers
- Young appear alert, though movement is not well coordinated
- Primary pins unsheathing

Feather Tract Development

Tract	N	V	P	U	F	n
Capital				100		10
Dorsal				100		10
Humeral				100		10
Alar				100		10
Femoral				100		10
Crural			20	80		10
Caudal				100		10
Ventral				100		10

Feather Tract Development

Tract	N	V	P	U	F	n
Capital				100		6
Dorsal				100		6
Humeral				100		6
Alar				100		6
Femoral				100		6
Crural				100		6
Caudal				100		6
Ventral				100		6

Morphometric Data

Measurements	Mean ± SD	Min	Max	n
Weight	9.85 ± 0.463	9.1	10.5	11
Tarsus	19.37 ± 1.696	16.97	22.73	12
Wing Chord	22.08 ± 2.712	19.0	28.0	12
Culmen	3.87 ± 0.428	3.29	4.55	10
Outer Primary	7.74 ± 1.402	6.0	10.0	12
Outer Rectrix	1.81 ± 1.269	0.5	5.0	12
Longest Broken Primary	1.5 ± 0.972	0	3.0	10
Length	52.6 ± 2.633	49.0	57.0	10
Gape	11.25 ± 0.485	10.49	11.79	10

Morphometric Data

Measurements	Mean ± SD	Min	Max	n
Weight	10.7 ± 0.544	10.0	11.4	6
Tarsus	20.50 ± 1.325	19.11	21.98	6
Wing Chord	24.67 ± 1.633	23.0	27.0	6
Culmen	3.93 ± 0.214	3.72	4.15	4
Outer Primary	8.44 ± 1.512	6.0	10.52	6
Outer Rectrix	2.85 ± 0.943	2.0	4.0	6
Longest Broken Primary	2.75 ± 0.957	2.0	4.0	4
Length	54.0 ± 1.826	52.0	56.0	4
Gape	10.96 ± 0.386	10.4	11.29	4

General Description

Eyes are open most of the time. Nestlings beginning to appear soft due to the extent of the unsheathed pin feathers. Bill darkening may begin to extend into the gape. All body pins continue to unsheathe. Primaries and secondaries may begin to unsheathe. P9 measures about 10 mm.

General Description

Eyes are open most of the time. Nestlings appear feathered with apteria mostly covered along back and flanks. Most alar pins are unsheathing. Body pins continue to unsheathe. P9 measures about 12 mm. Unsheathed portion of rectrices about 2 mm. Young are typically ready for banding.

Sprague's Pipit
Anthus spragueii
Data collection: Bowdoin National Wildlife Refuge, Phillips County, Montana. Nests: $n = 1$ (2004).
Nest Period Data: Average (range). n = number of nests
Building: No data
Clutch size: 4.6 (1 - 6) eggs, $n = 123$
Incubation: 12.2 (7 - 15) days, $n = 85$
Nestling: 13.1 (9 - 17) days, $n = 17$

Indicator Table: Sprague's Pipit visual characteristics typical at a given age.

Indicator characteristics	Age	Indicator characteristics	Age
No feather tracts visible below skin	1	Pin feathers emerged on all tracts	6
Feather tracts may be just visible as stippling on skin or small dark spots	2	Some tracts begin to unsheathe	7
No data	3	All tracts begin to unsheathe. Primaries begin to unsheathe	8
Eyes partially open. Alar tracts beginning to emerge	4	No data	9
Eyes appear fully open. Pin feathers are out on some tracts	5	Primaries are unsheathed about 1 mm	10
		Sheathes on most feather tracts no longer visible or obscured by feathers	11

General Feather Development: Sprague's Pipit feather tract development by day. Most advanced stage is indicated as N-Not visible (not pigmented), V-Visible below skin, P-Pins above skin, U-Unsheathing, or F-Fully unsheathed.

Day	Capital	Dorsal	Humeral	Alar	Femoral	Crural	Caudal	Ventral
1	N	N	N	N	N	N	N	N
2	V	V	V		V	N	N	V
3								
4	V	V	V	P	V	V	V	V
5	V	P	P	P	P	V	V	P
6	P	P	P	P	P	P	P	P
7	P	U	U	P	U	P	P	U
8	U	U	U	U	U	U	U	U
9								
10	U	U	U	U	U	U	U	U
11	U	U	U	U	U	U	U	U
12	U	U	U	U	U	U	U	U

Sprague's Pipit *(Anthus spragueii)* continued

Day 1 Key Visual Indicators:

- No feather tracts visible beneath skin
- Eyes closed
- Nestling may be curled into a ball

Day 2 Key Visual Indicators:

- Eyes closed
- Most feather tracts (except caudal and crural) becoming visible as stippling on skin or very small dark spots

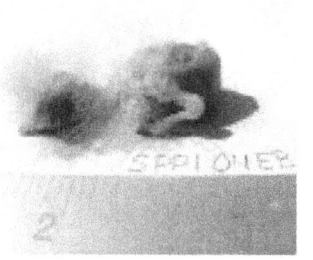

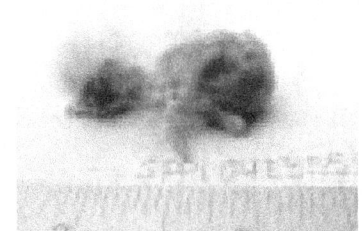

Feather Tract Development

Tract	N	V	P	U	F	n
Capital	100					2
Dorsal	100					2
Humeral	100					2
Alar	100					2
Femoral	100					2
Crural	100					2
Caudal	100					2
Ventral	100					2

Feather Tract Development

Tract	N	V	P	U	F	n
Capital		100				2
Dorsal		100				2
Humeral		100				2
Alar		100				2
Femoral		100				2
Crural	100					2
Caudal	100					2
Ventral		100				2

Morphometric Data

Measurements	Mean	Min	Max	n
Weight	2.5	2.2	2.8	2
Tarsus	6.59	6.00	7.19	2
Wing Chord	6.0	6.0	6.0	2
Culmen	2.17	2.08	2.27	2
Outer Primary	0	0	0	2
Outer Rectrix	0	0	0	2
Longest Broken Primary	0	0	0	2
Length	37.5	37.0	38.0	2
Gape	7.86	7.78	7.95	2

Morphometric Data

Measurements	Mean	Min	Max	n
Weight	3.3	3.3	3.4	2
Tarsus	7.81	7.76	7.86	2
Wing Chord	7.0	7.0	7.0	2
Culmen	2.39	2.32	2.46	2
Outer Primary	0	0	0	2
Outer Rectrix	0	0	0	2
Longest Broken Primary	0	0	0	2
Length	40.5	40.0	41.0	2
Gape	9.08	8.88	9.29	2

General Description

Skin and legs salmon colored. Long, light grey (almost white) down on most feather tracts but no tracts are visible beneath skin. Rictus yellow. Eyes closed. May display weak or shaky gaping. Can't hold head up. Lays flat on belly or may curl into ball shape. Quiet.

General Description

Appearance very much the same as Day 1. Most feather tracts (except caudal and crural) becoming visible as small dark spots under skin or stippling on skin surface. Eyes closed. More movement than Day 1 but still weak and shaky. Quiet.

Sprague's Pipit *(Anthus spragueii)* continued

Day 3 No data

Day 4 Key Visual Indicators:

- Eyes partially open
- All feather tracts visible with alar just beginning to emerge

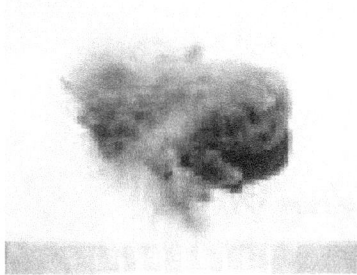

Feather Tract Development

Tract	N	V	P	U	F	*n*
Capital		100				2
Dorsal		100				2
Humeral		100				2
Alar			100			2
Femoral		100				2
Crural		100				2
Caudal		100				2
Ventral		100				2

Morphometric Data

Measurements	Mean	Min	Max	*n*
Weight	6.7	6.6	6.8	2
Tarsus	11.38	10.97	11.80	2
Wing Chord	11.0	10.0	12.0	2
Culmen	3.27	3.16	3.38	2
Outer Primary	0	0	0	2
Outer Rectrix	0	0	0	2
Longest Broken Primary	0	0	0	2
Length	48.5	48.0	49.0	2
Gape	11.38	10.94	11.82	2

General Description

Skin, legs and bill pink. Rictus yellow. Still downy. All tracts visible under skin. Alar tract just beginning to emerge. Eyes may be partially open. Movement is stronger but not held for long. One nestling made soft clicking noises.

Sprague's Pipit *(Anthus spragueii)* continued

Day 5 Key Visual Indicators:

- Eyes fully open
- Pin feathers on wings and most body tracts

Day 6 Key Visual Indicators:

- Pin feathers have emerged on all tracts

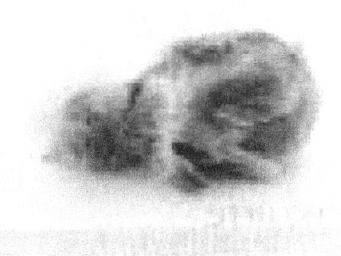

Feather Tract Development

Tract	N	V	P	U	F	n
Capital		100				2
Dorsal			100			2
Humeral			100			2
Alar			100			2
Femoral		50	50			2
Crural		100				2
Caudal		100				2
Ventral		50	50			2

Feather Tract Development

Tract	N	V	P	U	F	n
Capital			100			2
Dorsal			100			2
Humeral			100			2
Alar			100			2
Femoral			100			2
Crural			100			2
Caudal			100			2
Ventral			100			2

Morphometric Data

Measurements	Mean	Min	Max	n
Weight	8.0	7.8	8.3	2
Tarsus	13.47	13.18	13.76	2
Wing Chord	12.0	11.0	13.0	2
Culmen	3.50	3.49	3.52	2
Outer Primary	1.0	1.0	1.0	2
Outer Rectrix	0	0	0	2
Longest Broken Primary	0	0	0	2
Length	50.5	50.0	51.0	2
Gape	12.23	12.11	12.35	2

Morphometric Data

Measurements	Mean	Min	Max	n
Weight	11.7	11.2	12.2	2
Tarsus	15.75	15.33	16.17	2
Wing Chord	17.0	16.0	18.0	2
Culmen	3.92	3.88	3.97	2
Outer Primary	3.5	3.0	4.0	2
Outer Rectrix	0.5	0	1.0	2
Longest Broken Primary	0	0	0	2
Length	53.0	51.0	55.0	2
Gape	12.79	12.77	12.81	2

General Description

Eyes fully open. Pins emerging on dorsal, alar and humeral tracts and may be emerging on ventral and femoral. Not much movement, some gaping. Quiet.

General Description

Down on dorsal, capital and alar tracts. Down is approx. 10 mm long but getting more sparse. Pin feathers have emerged on all tracts, however caudal may be barely emerging. May balance on rump and tarsus. Soft clicking noises.

Sprague's Pipit *(Anthus spragueii)* continued

Day 7 Key Visual Indicators:

- Some feathers beginning to unsheathe

Day 8 Key Visual Indicators:

- All tracts unsheathing
- Primaries beginning to unsheathe

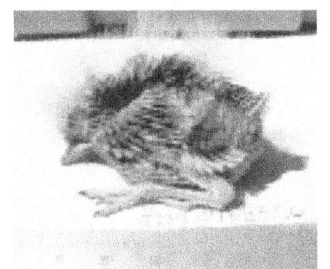

Feather Tract Development

Tract	N	V	P	U	F	n
Capital			100			2
Dorsal				100		2
Humeral			50	50		2
Alar			100			2
Femoral			50	50		2
Crural			100			2
Caudal			100			2
Ventral			50	50		2

Feather Tract Development

Tract	N	V	P	U	F	n
Capital				100		2
Dorsal				100		2
Humeral				100		2
Alar				100		2
Femoral				100		2
Crural				100		2
Caudal				100		2
Ventral				100		2

Morphometric Data

Measurements	Mean	Min	Max	n
Weight	13.4	12.9	14.0	2
Tarsus	18.13	17.90	18.36	2
Wing Chord	21.0	20.0	22.0	2
Culmen	4.35	4.14	4.57	2
Outer Primary	6.5	6.0	7.0	2
Outer Rectrix	1.5	1.0	2.0	2
Longest Broken Primary	0	0	0	2
Length	58.0	56.0	60.0	2
Gape	13.44	13.24	13.64	2

Morphometric Data

Measurements	Mean	Min	Max	n
Weight	15.0	13.9	16.1	2
Tarsus	19.79	19.71	19.88	2
Wing Chord	27.0	26.0	28.0	2
Culmen	4.54	4.47	4.62	2
Outer Primary	10.0	9.0	11.0	2
Outer Rectrix	3.5	3.0	4.0	2
Longest Broken Primary	0	0	0	2
Length	62.5	62.0	63.0	2
Gape	13.71	13.69	13.73	2

General Description

Sparse down on dorsal, capital and alar tracts. Dorsal pins unsheathing and possibly ventral, femoral and humeral. More alert. Makes soft clicking noises and occasionally a soft chirp.

General Description

Down same as Day 7. All feather tracts unsheathing. Primaries just beginning to unsheathe. May make soft clicking noises.

Day 9 No data

Day 10 Key Visual Indicators:

- Primary pins unsheathing about 1 mm

Feather Tract Development

Tract	N	V	P	U	F	*n*
Capital				100		2
Dorsal				100		2
Humeral				100		2
Alar				100		2
Femoral				100		2
Crural				100		2
Caudal				100		2
Ventral				100		2

Morphometric Data

Measurements	Mean	Min	Max	*n*
Weight	19.3	18.4	20.3	2
Tarsus	21.98	21.72	22.24	2
Wing Chord	36.5	34.0	39.0	2
Culmen	5.09	4.93	5.26	2
Outer Primary	17.0	15.0	19.0	2
Outer Rectrix	7.5	7.0	8.0	2
Longest Broken Primary	3.5	1.0	6.0	2
Length	76.0	75.0	77.0	2
Gape	13.86	13.76	13.96	2

General Description

Down still apparent on head and back and a little on the wings. Most feathers well out of sheaths except around the face. Primaries have emerged. Feathers on head and back dark, chest is brown and belly is tan/white. Much more active with some soft clicking and chirping.

Sprague's Pipit *(Anthus spragueii)* continued

Day 11 Key Visual Indicators:

- Sheaths on most feather tracts are no longer visible except on wings

Day 12 Key Visual Indicators:

- Appearance similar to Day 11
- Base of remiges in sheath, but obscured by exposed feathers

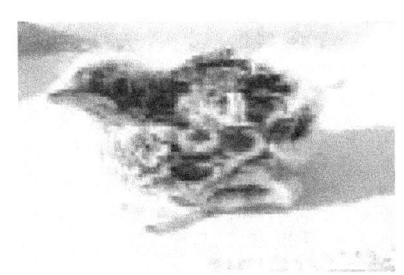

Feather Tract Development

Tract	N	V	P	U	F	n
Capital				100		2
Dorsal				100		2
Humeral				100		2
Alar				100		2
Femoral				100		2
Crural				100		2
Caudal				100		2
Ventral				100		2

Feather Tract Development

Tract	N	V	P	U	F	n
Capital				100		2
Dorsal				100		2
Humeral				100		2
Alar				100		2
Femoral				100		2
Crural				100		2
Caudal				100		2
Ventral				100		2

Morphometric Data

Measurements	Mean	Min	Max	n
Weight	18.8	18.3	19.4	2
Tarsus	22.4	22.3	22.5	2
Wing Chord	41.0	38.0	44.0	2
Culmen	5.22	5.18	5.27	2
Outer Primary	22.0	20.0	24.0	2
Outer Rectrix	9.5	9.0	10.0	2
Longest Broken Primary	6.0	3.0	9.0	2
Length	78.0	77.0	79.0	2
Gape	13.42	13.29	13.55	2

Morphometric Data

Measurements	Mean	Min	Max	n
Weight	19.0	18.1	20.0	2
Tarsus	22.82	22.57	23.08	2
Wing Chord	45.5	43.0	48.0	2
Culmen	5.61	5.33	5.89	2
Outer Primary	24.0	22.0	26.0	2
Outer Rectrix	10.5	10.0	11.0	2
Longest Broken Primary	13.0	12.0	14.0	2
Length				
Gape	13.24	13.12	13.36	2

General Description

Still some sparse down. Sheaths at bottom of all feathers but only visible on wings. Very active but quiet.

General Description

Down very sparse on back and head, almost gone from the wings. Base of remiges still in sheath, but obscured by exposed feathers. Very active, standing and jumping. Some chirping/squawking noises mostly while trying to escape.

Song Sparrow
Melospiza melodia gouldii
Data collection: Point Reyes National Seashore, Marin County, California. Nests: $n = 11$ (2004), $n = 9$ (2005).
Nest Period Data: Average (range), n = number of nests
Building: No data
Clutch size: 3 (2 - 5) eggs, $n = 198$
Incubation period: 13 (12 - 16) days, $n = 40$
Nestling period: 9 (8 - 12) days, $n = 55$

Indicator Table: Song Sparrow visual characteristics typical at a given age.

Indicator characteristics	Age	Indicator characteristics	Age
Alar pins in a band centered across wing	1	Eyes just beginning to open	5
Alar pins have grown towards posterior edge of wing	2	Some contour pins begin to unsheathe	5
Ventral tract appears as spots from furculum to mid chest	2	Eyes appear fully open	5-6
Some primary pins are just out	3	Primary pins beginning to unsheathe	7
All primary and secondary pins are out	3-4	All feather tracts are unsheathing	7-8
Outer primaries about 2mm long	4		

General Feather Development: Song Sparrow feather tract development by day. Most advanced stage is indicated as N-Not visible (not pigmented), V-Visible below skin, P-Pins above skin, U-Unsheathing, or F-Fully unsheathed.

Day	Capital	Dorsal	Humeral	Alar	Femoral	Crural	Caudal	Ventral
1	N V	N V	N V	V	N V	N V	N	N V
2	N V	V	N V	V P	N V	N V	N V	N V
3	V	V P	V P	V P	V P	N V	N V	V P
4	V P	V P	V P	P	V P	V P	V P	V P
5	V P	P U	P	P	V P	V P	V P	V P U
6	V P	P U	P U	P U	V P U	V P U	V P	P U
7	P U	P U	P U	P U	P U	P U	V P U	P U
8	U	U	U	U	U	U	P U	U

Song Sparrow *(Melospiza melodia gouldii)* continued

Day 1 Key Visual Indicators:

- Alar pins centered across wing and not individually distinguishable
- Young are small (egg size)
- Down may appear moist
- Egg tooth is prominent/visible

Day 2 Key Visual Indicators:

- Alar pins individually distinguishable
- Alar pins stretched towards posterior edge of wing

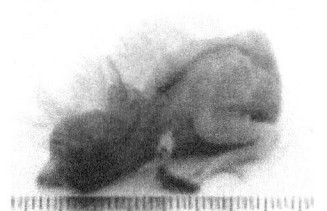

Feather Tract Development

Tract	N	V	P	U	F	n
Capital	60	40				20
Dorsal	5	95				20
Humeral	15	85				20
Alar		100				20
Femoral	80	20				20
Crural	95	5				20
Caudal	100					20
Ventral	70	30				20

Feather Tract Development

Tract	N	V	P	U	F	n
Capital	3	97				32
Dorsal		100				32
Humeral	3	97				32
Alar		97	3			32
Femoral	31	69				32
Crural	55	45				31
Caudal	68	32				31
Ventral	6	94				32

Morphometric Data

Measurements	Mean ± SD	Min	Max	n
Weight	2.28 ± 0.549	1.5	3.8	20
Tarsus	7.02 ± 0.944	5.64	9.04	20
Wing Chord	4.65 ± 0.671	4.0	6.5	20
Culmen	2.14 ± 0.228	1.84	2.9	20
Outer Primary	0	0	0	12
Outer Rectrix	0	0	0	12
Longest Broken Primary	0	0	0	20
Length	36.53 ± 4.128	28.0	46.0	19
Gape	7.46 ± 0.481	6.87	8.88	20

Morphometric Data

Measurements	Mean ± SD	Min	Max	n
Weight	3.434 ± 0.695	2.5	5.9	32
Tarsus	8.54 ± 1.018	6.06	10.46	32
Wing Chord	5.45 ± 0.766	4.0	8.0	32
Culmen	2.41 ± 0.303	1.42	2.83	32
Outer Primary	0.03 ± 0	0	0.5	16
Outer Rectrix	0	0	0	16
Longest Broken Primary	0	0	0	32
Length	38.91 ± 2.97	35.0	48.0	32
Gape	8.68 ± 0.746	7.23	10.02	32

General Description

Eyes closed. Ears are closed, though a small indentation is visible. Bill is orange/grey with, some brown at the tip and a yellowish/white rictus. The egg tooth is visible near the tip of the upper mandible. Skin is a light orange with some pink areas. Light gray down is present on capital, dorsal, alar, humeral, and femoral tracts. Eyelids appear large and dark gray. Ventral tract is visible as indentations on skin. Dorsal pins are visible as a very light gray stripe. Capital tract pins very light in color, small, and just visible. Femoral tract is typically not visible. Humeral tract is visible as a very light gray single line. Caudal and crural tracts are not visible. Young able to move all limbs very slowly and lift head briefly.

General Description

Eyes closed. Ears closed. Capital tract visible as gray flecks. Dorsal pins visible as gray flecks forming a stripe. Capital tract visible as gray flecks. Alar pins distinguishable as individual pins. Femoral tract is visible as a few gray flecks. Humeral tract is visible as a gray band. Caudal tract is visible as a single gray line. Crural tract is visible as a few gray flecks. Ventral tract is visible as gray spotting from furculum to about mid-chest; visible as skin markings posteriorly. May have small hair-like protrusions on wing where flight feathers will protrude. Young are able to quietly chirp and move all limbs.

Day 3 Key Visual Indicators:

- Some to all remiges emerging
- P9 measures about 1mm

Day 4 Key Visual Indicators:

- All remiges have emerged
- P9 measures about 2 mm
- Most body pins appear to be just out or pushing up on skin surface
- Eyes may be partially open

Feather Tract Development

Tract	N	V	P	U	F	n
Capital		100				30
Dorsal		97	3			30
Humeral		93	7			30
Alar		17	83			30
Femoral		93	7			30
Crural	7	93				30
Caudal	10	90				30
Ventral		97	3			30

Feather Tract Development

Tract	N	V	P	U	F	n
Capital		85	15			26
Dorsal		58	42			26
Humeral		46	54			26
Alar			100			26
Femoral		80	19			26
Crural		96	4			26
Caudal		96	4			26
Ventral		58	42			26

Morphometric Data

Measurements	Mean ± SD	Min	Max	n
Weight	5.45 ± 1.157	3.1	9.0	30
Tarsus	10.85 ± 1.417	8.63	14.37	30
Wing Chord	8.15 ± 1.885	5.0	12.0	30
Culmen	2.84 ± 0.273	2.3	3.57	30
Outer Primary	0.75 ± 0.429	0.5	2.0	18
Outer Rectrix	0	0	0	18
Longest Broken Primary	0	0	0	30
Length	42.5 ± 2.968	37.0	49.0	30
Gape	10.24 ± 0.820	7.98	11.77	30

Morphometric Data

Measurements	Mean ± SD	Min	Max	n
Weight	7.64 ± 1.495	3.6	10.3	25
Tarsus	13.44 ± 1.548	10.24	16.65	26
Wing Chord	11.94 ± 1.899	8.0	17.0	26
Culmen	3.27 ± 0.285	2.68	3.96	26
Outer Primary	2.25 ± 0.913	1.0	4.5	16
Outer Rectrix	0	0	0	16
Longest Broken Primary	0	0	0	26
Length	48.0 ± 3.544	40.0	55.0	26
Gape	11.25 ± 0.626	9.53	12.02	26

General Description

Eyes closed. Ears closed. Capital tract visible as gray flecks in a band with smaller flecks around the ear. Dorsal pins are visible as a gray stripe. Some or all remiges are emerging. P9 is less than 1mm. Humeral and femoral tracts darker, still not out. Caudal tract line a bit thicker. Crural tract pins visible as flecks, still not out. Ventral tract is visible as gray flecks from furculum to mid-chest. Some spotting on chin is visible. Pins along belly are light in color and still not out. Young lifting whole body and head up with forelimbs and legs.

General Description

Eyes may partially open. Ears open. Most body pins appear to be out or pushing up against the skin surface. A few femoral pins may be out or pushing on skin. Humeral pins are out. All other pins are pushing up on the skin except for the crural tract. All remiges have emerged. P9 measures about 2mm. Ventral pins may be just out or pushing on skin and much more pronounced. Skin color becoming darker pink. Down is still present. Young are able to turn over on to back.

Song Sparrow *(Melospiza melodia gouldii)* continued

Day 5 Key Visual Indicators:

- P9 measures about 4mm
- Most pin feathers are out
- Some body pins may begin unsheathing

Day 6 Key Visual Indicators:

- P9 measures about 6mm
- All dorsal pins are out

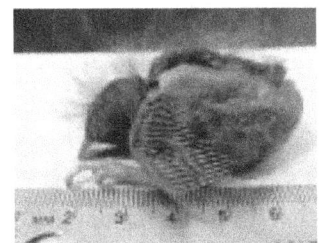

Feather Tract Development

Tract	N	V	P	U	F	n
Capital		50	50			26
Dorsal			96	4		26
Humeral			100			26
Alar			100			26
Femoral		4	96			26
Crural		58	42			26
Caudal		85	15			26
Ventral		4	92	4		26

Feather Tract Development

Tract	N	V	P	U	F	n
Capital		4	96			26
Dorsal			62	38		26
Humeral			54	46		26
Alar			92	8		26
Femoral		4	42	54		26
Crural		4	73	23		26
Caudal		23	77			26
Ventral			35	65		26

Morphometric Data

Measurements	Mean ± SD	Min	Max	n
Weight	9.86 ± 1.757	6.0	13.2	21
Tarsus	15.17 ± 1.549	11.44	18.04	26
Wing Chord	15.48 ± 2.012	11.0	22.0	26
Culmen	3.58 ± 0.306	3.02	4.18	26
Outer Primary	4.0 ± 1.676	2.0	8.0	14
Outer Rectrix	0.071 ± 0.182	0	0.5	14
Longest Broken Primary	0	0	0	26
Length	50.75 ± 2.625	46.0	56.0	24
Gape	11.95 ± 0.597	10.7	13.08	26

Morphometric Data

Measurements	Mean ± SD	Min	Max	n
Weight	11.73 ± 2.396	3.3	14.7	26
Tarsus	17.62 ± 2.032	12.05	20.74	26
Wing Chord	19.92 ± 3.215	11.0	24.0	26
Culmen	3.92 ± 0.404	2.91	4.62	26
Outer Primary	7.43 ± 2.065	3.5	10.0	14
Outer Rectrix	1.07 ± 0.829	0	2.0	14
Longest Broken Primary	0.038 ± 0.196	0	1.0	26
Length	54.46 ± 4.101	42.0	65.0	26
Gape	12.30 ± 0.744	9.97	13.31	26

General Description

Eyes may be opened partially. Capital tract pins are just out. Dorsal pins are out from nape to about mid-back. Some crural tract pins are out. Humeral and femoral pins are out 1 - 2 mm. Caudal tract shows hair-like projections where the rectrices will emerge. Ventral pins are out about 1 mm. P9 measures about 4 mm. Small subcutaneous pins are visible around ear and cloaca.

General Description

Eyes open. Capital tract pins are out about 1mm. Dorsal pins are out from nape to tail bud. Most crural tract pins are out. Humeral and femoral pins are out about 2 mm. Pins around ear are just emerging. Rectrices may be just emerging. Ventral pins are out about 2 mm. P9 measures about 6 mm. Tips of primaries may appear whitish and ready to break

Song Sparrow *(Melospiza melodia gouldii)* continued

Day 7 Key Visual Indicators:

- Flight feathers have begun to unsheathe
- All feather tracts are unsheathing
- Eyes may appear fully open

Feather Tract Development

Tract	N	V	P	U	F	*n*
Capital			56	44		25
Dorsal			8	92		25
Humeral			4	96		25
Alar			24	76		25
Femoral			4	96		25
Crural			28	72		25
Caudal		8	56	36		25
Ventral			4	96		25

Morphometric Data

Measurements	Mean ± SD	Min	Max	*n*
Weight	13.80 ± 1.641	9.2	15.7	26
Tarsus	19.66 ± 1.778	14.85	22.13	27
Wing Chord	24.35 ± 3.059	17.0	30.0	26
Culmen	4.38 ± 0.333	3.7	5.05	27
Outer Primary	10.69 ± 2.462	5.0	15.0	16
Outer Rectrix	2.91 ± 1.725	0	6.0	16
Longest Broken Primary	0.796 ± 1.031	0	4.0	27
Length	58.13 ± 4.174	54.0	70.0	24
Gape	12.34 ± 0.535	11.13	13.36	27

General Description

Dorsal pins are about 30% unsheathing. Capital tract pins are about 2 mm. Some crural pins are unsheathing. Some femoral pins are unsheathing. Most humeral pins are unsheathing. Flight feathers have begun to unsheathe. Ventral pins are mostly unsheathed with the exception of the throat area. Young are typically ready for banding. Young are prone to "jump" after this day.

Chestnut-collared Longspur
Calcarius ornatus
Data collection: Bowdoin National Wildlife Refuge, Phillips County, Montana. Nests: $n = 1$ (2004), $n = 1$ (2005), $n = 5$ (2006)
Nest Period Data: Average (range), n = number of nests
Building: no data
Clutch size: 4.1 (1 - 7) eggs, $n = 764$
Incubation: 11.0 (7 - 15) days, $n = 553$
Nestling: 11.3 (7 - 15) days, $n = 166$

Indicator Table: Chestnut-collared Longspur visual characteristics typical at a given age.

Indicator characteristics	Age	Indicator characteristics	Age
No feather tracts are visible	1	Pin feathers have emerged on all tracts	5
Alar, dorsal, and ventral tracts becoming visible	2	Pins begin to unsheathe. Primary tips pale and ready to unsheathe	6
Alar pins have grown towards posterior edge of wing and pressing on skin surface	3	Primary pins begin to unsheathe	7
Eyes begin to open. Alar pins typically emerged	4	All feather tracts are unsheathing	8

General Feather Development: Chestnut-collared Longspur feather tract development by day. Most advanced stage is indicated as N-Not visible (not pigmented), V-Visible below skin, P-Pins above skin, U-Unsheathing, or F-Fully unsheathed.

Day	Capital	Dorsal	Humeral	Alar	Femoral	Crural	Caudal	Ventral
1	N	N	N	N	N	N	N	N V
2	N	N V	N	N V	N	N	N	N V
3	N V	N V	N V	N V P	N V	N V	N V	V P
4	N V	N V P	N V P	N V P	V P	N V P	N V P	V P
5	N V P	V P	V P	V P	V P	N V P	N V P	V P
6	V P U	P U	P U	P U	P U	V P U	V P	P U
7	P U	P U	P U	P U	U	P U	P U	P U
8	U	U	U	U	U	U	U	U

Day 1 Key Visual Indicators:

- Down may appear wet or clumped together
- Eyes closed
- Nestling may be curled into a ball

Day 2 Key Visual Indicators:

- Some feather tracts (alar, dorsal, and ventral) becoming visible as darker areas or very small dark spots

Feather Tract Development

Tract	N	V	P	U	F	n
Capital	100					8
Dorsal	100					8
Humeral	100					8
Alar	100					8
Femoral	100					8
Crural	100					8
Caudal	100					8
Ventral	88	12				8

Feather Tract Development

Tract	N	V	P	U	F	n
Capital	100					10
Dorsal	60	40				10
Humeral	100					10
Alar	50	50				10
Femoral	100					10
Crural	100					10
Caudal	100					10
Ventral	40	60				10

Morphometric Data

Measurements	Mean ± SD	Min	Max	n
Weight	2.12 ± 0.41	1.7	2.8	9
Tarsus	6.75 ± 0.67	5.93	7.94	9
Wing Chord	5.78 ± 0.87	4.5	7.0	9
Culmen	2.29 ± 0.14	2.1	2.5	9
Outer Primary	0	0	0	10
Outer Rectrix	0	0	0	10
Longest Broken Primary	0	0	0	10
Length	35.0 ± 1.91	33.0	38.0	7
Gape	7.92 ± 0.74	6.85	8.9	7

Morphometric Data

Measurements	Mean ± SD	Min	Max	n
Weight	3.16 ± 0.78	1.9	4.7	10
Tarsus	7.90 ± 0.69	6.62	8.91	10
Wing Chord	6.96 ± 1.34	4.9	9.0	8
Culmen	2.50 ± 0.29	1.82	2.8	9
Outer Primary	0	0	0	9
Outer Rectrix	0	0	0	10
Longest Broken Primary	0	0	0	10
Length	38.7 ± 1.83	37.0	43.0	10
Gape	8.66 ± 0.69	7.4	9.77	10

General Description

Eyes and ears are closed. Skin and legs flesh colored with orange tinge (salmon). All feather tracts are usually not visible though areas around feather tracts may appear slightly darker or as stippling of skin surface. Skin lighter on ventral side and legs. Light grey/tan down on all feather tracts except ventral. Down approx. 5 mm long and may be wet or clumped together. Pale bill with white rictus. Ear canal appears as a shallow indentation. May display weak, shaky gaping and weak forward movement. Can't hold head up. Lays flat on belly or may curl into ball shape. Very rarely makes very soft chirping sound, most made no noise.

General Description

Appearance very much the same as first day except that skin appears slightly darker and some pins are becoming visible. Subcutaneous alar pins are becoming visible. Dorsal tract may be visible as darker area or very small dark spots. Ventral pins not pigmented. Position and movement the same as day one. Can't hold head up and may still curl into ball shape.

Chestnut-collared Longspur *(Calcarius ornatus)* continued

Day 3 Key Visual Indicators:

- Dorsal and capital tracts becoming darker (gray)
- Pins may be emerging on alar tract

Day 4 Key Visual Indicators:

- Eyes begin to open
- Most feather tracts visible
- Alar pins have typically emerged 1-2 mm

Feather Tract Development

Tract	N	V	P	U	F	*n*
Capital	15	85				13
Dorsal	8	92				13
Humeral	31	69				13
Alar	15	54	31			13
Femoral	31	69				13
Crural	54	46				13
Caudal	77	23				13
Ventral		92	8			13

Feather Tract Development

Tract	N	V	P	U	F	*n*
Capital	9	91				11
Dorsal		54	45			11
Humeral	9	55	36			11
Alar		18	82			11
Femoral		64	36			11
Crural	28	36	36			11
Caudal	27	64	9			11
Ventral		64	36			11

Morphometric Data

Measurements	Mean ± SD	Min	Max	*n*
Weight	4.49 ± 0.84	2.6	5.9	13
Tarsus	9.51 ± 1.05	6.89	11.19	13
Wing Chord	8.3 ± 1.10	6.5	10.3	13
Culmen	2.90 ± 0.34	2.25	3.4	13
Outer Primary	0.25 ± 0.45	0	1.0	12
Outer Rectrix	0	0	0	13
Longest Broken Primary	0	0	0	13
Length	43.45 ± 2.34	39.0	48.0	11
Gape	9.82 ± 0.71	8.19	10.93	13

Morphometric Data

Measurements	Mean ± SD	Min	Max	*n*
Weight	6.43 ± 1.31	3.7	8.5	11
Tarsus	11.50 ± 1.37	8.64	13.36	11
Wing Chord	11.5 ± 2.17	9.0	16.0	10
Culmen	3.28 ± 0.34	2.6	3.7	11
Outer Primary	1.56 ± 0.82	0.5	3.0	8
Outer Rectrix	0	0	0	13
Longest Broken Primary	0	0	0	13
Length	48.44 ± 3.32	41.0	53.0	9
Gape	10.81 ± 0.76	9.2	11.81	11

General Description

Eyes are closed. Ear canal is larger. Skin less orange and darker overall with dark gray areas at feather tracts. Pins may be emerging on alar tracts. Dorsal and capital tracts becoming darker gray. Dorsal tract forms a dark gray stripe along back. Ventral tract is clearly visible and may be pressing up on skin. Gape orange-red with white rictus. May be gaping at noises and holds head up for a few seconds. Movement weak but steadier. Can right itself with some effort. Quiet.

General Description

Eyes may be partially open. Ear canal appears open. Skin around dorsal tract appears reddish. Ventral side and legs flesh colored. All feather tracts except caudal are visible and may be pressing up on skin. Alar pins have typically emerged. Still downy on all tracts except ventral; caudal down very sparse or absent. Gaping longer and overall movement is stronger. Rights itself in a few seconds and weakly scoots forward with legs. Some soft noises including soft clicking noises.

Day 5 Key Visual Indicators:

- Eyes partially to fully open
- Pin feathers are typically out on all tracts
- Movement is strong and nestling may balance on rump and tarsus

Day 6 Key Visual Indicators:

- Pins may be unsheathing on all feather tracts except caudal
- Eyes may appear fully open
- Primary tips appear pale and ready to unsheathe

Feather Tract Development

Tract	N	V	P	U	F	n
Capital	8	23	69			13
Dorsal		15	85			13
Humeral		15	85			13
Alar		8	92			13
Femoral		15	85			13
Crural	15	15	70			13
Caudal	8	30	62			13
Ventral		31	69			13

Feather Tract Development

Tract	N	V	P	U	F	n
Capital		9	82	9		11
Dorsal			64	36		11
Humeral			55	45		11
Alar			64	36		11
Femoral			36	64		11
Crural		9	64	27		11
Caudal		9	91			11
Ventral			55	45		11

Morphometric Data

Measurements	Mean ± SD	Min	Max	n
Weight	8.88 ± 1.29	6.2	11.2	13
Tarsus	14.09 ± 1.21	12.26	15.77	13
Wing Chord	16.27 ± 2.57	11.0	21.5	13
Culmen	3.74 ± 0.23	3.38	4.1	13
Outer Primary	3.95 ± 2.31	1.5	9.0	10
Outer Rectrix	0.35 ± 0.55	0	1.5	13
Longest Broken Primary	0	0	0	13
Length	53.91 ± 1.51	51.0	56.0	11
Gape	11.73 ± 0.65	10.3	12.8	13

Morphometric Data

Measurements	Mean ± SD	Min	Max	n
Weight	10.18 ± 1.56	7.7	11.7	11
Tarsus	15.76 ± 1.34	12.86	17.33	11
Wing Chord	20.18 ± 2.48	16.0	23.0	11
Culmen	4.03 ± 0.31	3.58	4.6	11
Outer Primary	6.73 ± 1.79	4.0	9.0	11
Outer Rectrix	1.09 ± 0.70	0	2.0	11
Longest Broken Primary	0	0	0	11
Length	58.11 ± 3.22	55.0	66.0	9
Gape	12.37 ± 0.63	11.08	13.13	11

General Description

Eyes at least partially open. Skin appears the same color as day four. Pins are typically emerging on all feather tracts but unsheathing has not yet begun. Down still present but more sparse. More frequent, stronger movement and may balance on rump and tarsus. More frequent and louder chirping noises.

General Description

Eyes are fully open. Feathers may be beginning to unsheathe on all tracts except caudal and capital. Tips of primaries appear pale and ready to unsheathe. Tips of wing coverts may appear tan colored if unsheathed. Down still present. Movement is strong, holds head up. Makes chirping noises as well as occasional harsher, louder chips.

Chestnut-collared Longspur *(Calcarius ornatus)* continued

Day 7 Key Visual Indicators:

- Primaries may begin to unsheathe
- Holds head up almost constantly

Day 8 Key Visual Indicators:

- Primaries unsheathing 2-3 mm
- All feather tracts are unsheathing

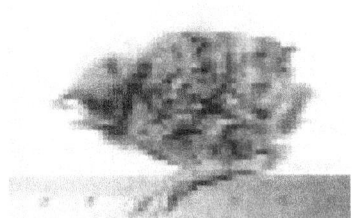

Feather Tract Development

Tract	N	V	P	U	F	n
Capital			45	55		9
Dorsal			22	88		9
Humeral			45	55		9
Alar			11	89		9
Femoral				100		9
Crural			22	78		9
Caudal			78	22		9
Ventral			11	89		9

Feather Tract Development

Tract	N	V	P	U	F	n
Capital				100		4
Dorsal				100		4
Humeral				100		4
Alar				100		4
Femoral				100		4
Crural				100		4
Caudal				100		4
Ventral				100		4

Morphometric Data

Measurements	Mean ± SD	Min	Max	n
Weight	12.01 ± 2.85	7.0	14.7	9
Tarsus	17.76 ± 1.41	15.2	19.69	9
Wing Chord	25.33 ± 4.85	18.0	33.0	9
Culmen	4.39 ± 0.36	3.8	4.9	9
Outer Primary	10.22 ± 2.28	7.0	14.0	9
Outer Rectrix	2.67 ± 1.22	1.0	5.0	9
Longest Broken Primary	0.44 ± 0.53	0	1.0	9
Length	63.71 ± 4.96	58.0	70.0	7
Gape	12.40 ± 0.61	11.33	13.27	9

Morphometric Data

Measurements	Mean ± SD	Min	Max	n
Weight	14.9 ± 0.90	14	16.1	4
Tarsus	18.98 ± 0.68	18.06	19.65	4
Wing Chord	31.0 ± 3.27	27.0	35.0	4
Culmen	4.52 ± 0.27	4.26	4.8	4
Outer Primary	13.5 ± 2.52	10.0	16.0	4
Outer Rectrix	3.75 ± 0.50	3.0	4.0	4
Longest Broken Primary	2.25 ± 0.96	1.0	3.0	4
Length	67.75 ± 5.91	60.0	74.0	4
Gape	12.48 ± 0.21	12.18	12.68	4

General Description

Sparse down. All feather tracts are typically unsheathing except caudal. Primaries are beginning to unsheathe. Apteria are obscured by pin feathers along back and flanks. Moves more frequently and appears alert. Holds head up almost constantly. Young are typically ready for banding.

General Description

All feather tracts unsheathing. Primaries typically unsheathed 2-3 mm. Unsheathed wing coverts form light tan wing bars. Most feathers out to the extent that sheaths may not be visible under feathers and young appear feathered. More active, controlled movements and chirping noises given.

American Goldfinch
Cardeulis tristis
Data collection: Point Reyes National Seashore, Marin County, California. Nests: $n = 4$ (2004), $n = 2$ (2005).
Nest Period Data: Average (range), n = number of nests
Building: no data
Clutch size: 4.9 (4 - 6) eggs, $n = 55$
Incubation: 11.5 (10 - 17) days, $n = 16$
Nestling: 13.5 (11 - 16) days, $n = 15$

Indicator Table: American Goldfinch visual characteristics typical at a given age.

Indicator characteristics	Age	Indicator characteristics	Age
Alar pins are very light in color and difficult to see	1	Contour feather pins begin to emerge	6
Alar pins are light in color and centered across the dorsal wing surface	2	Ventral tract has begun to unsheathe	7
		Most contour feather tracts have begun to unsheathe	8
Dorsal tract is visible as light gray pins	3	Primary pins begin to unsheathe	8-9
Eyes begin to open	4-5	Capital tract pins are unsheathing	10
Alar pins have grown to posterior edge of wing and appear ready to emerge	4	Young appear soft due to extent of unsheathing	11
Alar pins begin to emerge	5	Young appear very alert and can hop on the ground	11

General Feather Development: American Goldfinch feather tract development by day. Most advanced stage is indicated as N-Not visible (not pigmented), V-Visible below skin, P-Pins above skin, U-Unsheathing, or F-Fully unsheathed.

Day	Capital	Dorsal	Humeral	Alar	Femoral	Crural	Caudal	Ventral
1	N	N	N	N V	N	N	N	N
2	N	N V	N V	V	N	N	N	N
3	N V	N V	N V	V	N V	N	N V	N V
4	V	V	V	V	V	N V	N V	V
5	V	V	V	P	V	V	V	V P
6	V	V P	V P	P	V P	V P	V P	V P
7	V P	P	P	P	P U	V P	V P	P U
8	P	P U	P U	P U	U	P U	P U	U
9	P U	U	U	U	U	U	P U	U
10	U	U	U	U	U	U	U	U
11	U	U	U	U	U	U	U	U

American Goldfinch *(Cardeulis tristis)* continued

Day 1 Key Visual Indicators:

- Young are egg size and down may be matted
- Alar pins are very light in color and difficult to see
- No other pigmented pins are visible

Day 2 Key Visual Indicators:

- Alar pins are light in color and centered across the dorsal surface of wing
- No other feather tracts are readily apparent

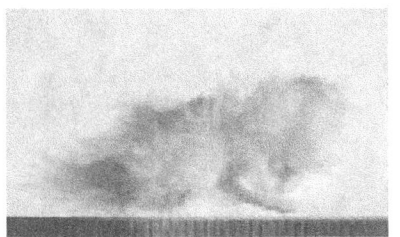

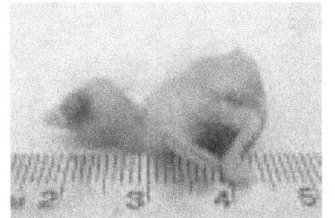

Feather Tract Development

Tract	N	V	P	U	F	n
Capital	100					6
Dorsal	100					6
Humeral	100					6
Alar	33	67				6
Femoral	100					6
Crural	100					6
Caudal	100					6
Ventral	100					6

Feather Tract Development

Tract	N	V	P	U	F	n
Capital	100					8
Dorsal	75	25				8
Humeral	87.5	12.5				8
Alar		100				8
Femoral	100					8
Crural	100					8
Caudal	100					8
Ventral	100					7

Morphometric Data

Measurements	Mean ± SD	Min	Max	n
Weight	1.23 ± 0.288	0.8	1.6	6
Tarsus	4.34 ± 0.214	4.13	4.67	6
Wing Chord	4.0 ± 0.316	3.5	4.5	6
Culmen	2.08 ± 0.117	1.91	2.21	6
Outer Primary	0	0	0	6
Outer Rectrix	0	0	0	6
Longest Broken Primary	0	0	0	6
Length	29.08 ± 2.764	25.5	33	6
Gape	5.64 ± 0.297	5.15	5.97	6

Morphometric Data

Measurements	Mean ± SD	Min	Max	n
Weight	2.05 ± 0.307	1.6	2.5	8
Tarsus	5.25 ± 0.406	4.6	5.72	8
Wing Chord	4.69 ± 0.372	0	5.0	8
Culmen	2.39 ± 0.076	2.32	2.52	8
Outer Primary	0	0	0	8
Outer Rectrix	0	0	0	8
Longest Broken Primary	0	0	0	8
Length	32.88 ± 2.031	31.0	36.0	8
Gape	6.55 ± 0.422	6.01	7.22	8

General Description

Eyes are closed. Ear is closed and visible as an indentation. Bill is yellow-orange with a violet-pink gape. Light colored down is present on the capital, dorsal, humeral, alar, femoral, and crural tracts and may be matted. Alar pins may be visible but are very light in color. No other feather tracts are visible. Young are egg size and weigh less than 2 grams.

General Description

Eyes are closed. Alar pins are visible as very light pins centered across the dorsal surface of wing. Ventral tract is not pigmented but appears as stippling on skin surface. No other tracts are visible.

Day 3 Key Visual Indicators:

- Alar pins have grown towards posterior edge of wing
- Dorsal tract is visible as very light gray pins
- Skin around head and dorsal surface begins to darken

Feather Tract Development

Tract	N	V	P	U	F	n
Capital	80	20				10
Dorsal	10	90				10
Humeral	50	50				10
Alar		100				10
Femoral	60	40				10
Crural	100					10
Caudal	60	40				10
Ventral	70	30				10

Morphometric Data

Measurements	Mean ± SD	Min	Max	n
Weight	2.58 ± 0.437	1.6	3	8
Tarsus	7.01 ± 1.026	5.92	8.94	10
Wing Chord	5.2 ± 1.033	3.0	6.0	10
Culmen	2.76 ± 0.127	2.55	2.99	10
Outer Primary	0	0	0	10
Outer Rectrix	0	0	0	10
Longest Broken Primary	0	0	0	10
Length	36.9 ± 2.283	32.0	40.0	10
Gape	7.08 ± 0.409	6.48	7.56	10

General Description

Eyes closed. Alar pins have grown towards posterior edge of wing. Dorsal tract is visible as light gray pins. Humeral tract may be visible. Caudal tract may just be visible. Ventral tract is visible as unpigmented stippling. Abdomen is enlarged and darkening.

Day 4 Key Visual Indicators:

- Alar pins have grown to the posterior edge of wing and appear ready to emerge
- Hair-like projections appear where alar pins will emerge

Feather Tract Development

Tract	N	V	P	U	F	n
Capital		100				6
Dorsal		100				6
Humeral		100				6
Alar		100				6
Femoral		100				6
Crural	67	33				6
Caudal	17	83				6
Ventral		100				6

Morphometric Data

Measurements	Mean ± SD	Min	Max	n
Weight	3.54 ± 0.688	2.4	4.1	5
Tarsus	8.95 ± 0.830	7.44	9.85	6
Wing Chord	6.92 ± 0.970	5.0	7.5	6
Culmen	3.11 ± 0.111	2.92	3.24	6
Outer Primary	0	0	0	6
Outer Rectrix	0	0	0	6
Longest Broken Primary	0	0	0	6
Length	41.67 ± 2.875	37.0	45.0	6
Gape	8.03 ± 0.654	6.74	8.51	6

General Description

Eyes may be partially opened. Ear canal may be partially open. Capital tract is just becoming visible and area is darkening. Dorsal tract area is darkening. Alar pins have grown to the edge of wing and appear ready to emerge. Hair-like projections appear where alar pins will emerge. Humeral tract visible as gray flecks. Ventral tract visible as gray flecks near the chest and as flesh colored stippling across the sides of the abdomen.

American Goldfinch *(Cardeulis tristis)* continued

Day 5 Key Visual Indicators:

- Alar tract pins have emerged or just emerged
- Capital, dorsal, and humeral tracts are dark, but no pins have emerged

Feather Tract Development

Tract	N	V	P	U	F	*n*
Capital		100				8
Dorsal		100				8
Humeral		100				8
Alar			100			8
Femoral		100				8
Crural		100				8
Caudal		100				8
Ventral		87.5	12.5			8

Morphometric Data

Measurements	Mean ± SD	Min	Max	*n*
Weight	5.11 ± 0.582	4.4	6.2	8
Tarsus	10.19 ± 1.288	8.43	12.12	8
Wing Chord	11.38 ± 1.706	8.0	14.0	8
Culmen	3.55 ± 0.088	3.34	3.63	8
Outer Primary	0.94 ± 0.417	0.5	1.5	8
Outer Rectrix	0	0	0	8
Longest Broken Primary	0	0	0	8
Length	45.38 ± 3.114	41.0	51.0	8
Gape	8.49 ± 0.295	8.13	8.99	8

General Description

Eyes are partially open. Capital tract is dark. Dorsal tract is dark and appears as a gray strip along the spine. Humeral and femoral tracts visible as a gray strip. Some alar pins have emerged. Crural tract visible as a few gray flecks. Seed stored in crop may be apparent.

Day 6 Key Visual Indicators:

- Alar pins are 2-3mm in length
- Most contour feather pins have just emerged or have tips pressing up on skin surface

Feather Tract Development

Tract	N	V	P	U	F	*n*
Capital		100				10
Dorsal		30	70			10
Humeral		30	70			10
Alar			100			10
Femoral		30	70			10
Crural		90	10			10
Caudal		90	10			10
Ventral		30	70			10

Morphometric Data

Measurements	Mean ± SD	Min	Max	*n*
Weight	6.09 ± 0.723	4.4	7.1	10
Tarsus	11.60 ± 0.774	10.37	12.96	10
Wing Chord	15.15 ± 1.717	11.0	17.0	10
Culmen	3.85 ± 0.199	3.45	4.15	10
Outer Primary	2.85 ± 0.883	0.5	3.5	10
Outer Rectrix	0.05 ± 0.158	0	0.5	10
Longest Broken Primary	0	0	0	10
Length	48.35 ± 3.496	41.0	54.0	10
Gape	8.82 ± 0.288	8.34	9.22	10

General Description

Dorsal, humeral, femoral, and ventral tracts have darkened and are just emerging. Primary, secondary, and some covert alar pins have emerged. Alar pins have emerged 2-3mm. Femoral pins have lengthened and may have emerged. Hair-like projections appear where caudal pins will emerge.

Day 7 Key Visual Indicators:

- Dorsal, humeral, and caudal tracts have emerged by 1-2 mm
- Ventral tract has just begun to unsheathe

Day 8 Key Visual Indicators:

- Some wing coverts have begun to unsheathe
- Capital tract pins have typically begun to emerge
- Most contour feather tracts have begun to un sheathe

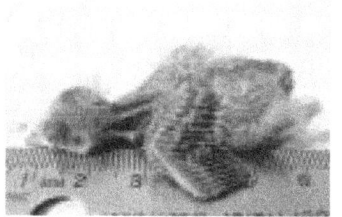

Feather Tract Development

Tract	N	V	P	U	F	n
Capital		87.5	12.5			8
Dorsal			100			8
Humeral			100			8
Alar			100			8
Femoral			75	25		8
Crural		12.5	87.5			8
Caudal		12.5	87.5			8
Ventral			37.5	62.5		8

Feather Tract Development

Tract	N	V	P	U	F	n
Capital			100			10
Dorsal			10	90		10
Humeral			10	90		10
Alar			20	80		10
Femoral				100		10
Crural			10	90		10
Caudal			80	20		10
Ventral				100		10

Morphometric Data

Measurements	Mean ± SD	Min	Max	n
Weight	7.03 ± 0.634	5.8	7.8	8
Tarsus	13.09 ± 0.731	12.27	14.64	8
Wing Chord	19.19 ± 1.963	15.0	21.5	8
Culmen	4.10 ± 0.156	3.76	4.25	8
Outer Primary	5.5 ± 1.282	2.5	6.5	8
Outer Rectrix	0.688 ± 0.372	0	1.0	8
Longest Broken Primary	0	0	0	8
Length	51.13 ± 4.581	42.0	58.0	8
Gape	8.99 ± 0.582	7.91	9.59	8

Morphometric Data

Measurements	Mean ± SD	Min	Max	n
Weight	8.34 ± 0.938	6.2	9.8	10
Tarsus	13.19 ± 0.721	11.96	14.23	10
Wing Chord	23.65 ± 2.310	18.0	26.0	10
Culmen	4.48 ± 0.201	4.19	4.87	10
Outer Primary	8.7 ± 1.418	5.0	10.0	10
Outer Rectrix	1.95 ± 0.762	0.5	3.0	10
Longest Broken Primary	0.25 ± 0.354	0	1.0	10
Length	55.5 ± 3.274	48.0	59.0	10
Gape	9.17 ± 0.650	8.01	9.95	10

General Description

Eyes appear fully open. Capital tract pushing up on skin. All other tracts have emerged. Dorsal and humeral tract pins are out 1-2 mm. Ventral pins are typically unsheathing. Caudal pins are just emerged.

General Description

Capital tract pins have emerged. Some dorsal, humeral, femoral, and crural tract pins unsheathing. Some wing coverts unsheathing. Primary and secondary pin tips appear white and ready to unsheathe or have just begun to unsheathe. Most ventral tract pins are unsheathing. Young can stand up on tarsus. Young are typically ready for banding.

American Goldfinch *(Cardeulis tristis)* continued

Day 9 Key Visual Indicators:

- Most primary pins have begun to unsheathe
- Most contour feather pins (except capital) are unsheathing at tips

Day 10 Key Visual Indicators:

- Capital tract pins are unsheathing at the tips
- Primary pins unsheathed 4-6 mm

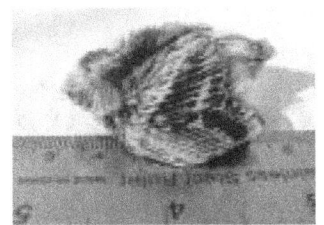

Feather Tract Development

Tract	N	V	P	U	F	*n*
Capital			50	50		8
Dorsal				100		8
Humeral				100		8
Alar				100		8
Femoral				100		8
Crural				100		8
Caudal		12.5		87.5		8
Ventral				100		8

Feather Tract Development

Tract	N	V	P	U	F	*n*
Capital				100		8
Dorsal				100		8
Humeral				100		8
Alar				100		8
Femoral				100		8
Crural				100		8
Caudal				100		8
Ventral				100		8

Morphometric Data

Measurements	Mean ± SD	Min	Max	*n*
Weight	9.09 ± 0.869	7.5	10.2	8
Tarsus	14.15 ± 0.669	13.54	15.19	7
Wing Chord	26.19 ± 2.137	22.0	29.0	8
Culmen	4.64 ± 0.180	4.3	4.91	8
Outer Primary	11.69 ± 1.624	8.0	13.0	8
Outer Rectrix	3.63 ± 1.188	1.0	5.0	8
Longest Broken Primary	1.56 ± 0.729	0	2.0	8
Length	57.25 ± 3.775	52.0	60.0	4
Gape	9.36 ± 0.447	8.94	10.14	8

Morphometric Data

Measurements	Mean ± SD	Min	Max	*n*
Weight	10.26 ± 0.898	8.6	11.5	8
Tarsus	14.32 ± 0.481	13.81	15.11	8
Wing Chord	30.69 ± 2.187	26.0	33.0	8
Culmen	4.91 ± 0.244	4.58	5.32	8
Outer Primary	15.0 ± 1.581	11.5	16.0	8
Outer Rectrix	5.69 ± 1.280	3.0	7.0	8
Longest Broken Primary	5.13 ± 1.356	3.0	7.0	8
Length	61.5 ± 3.786	56.0	64.0	4
Gape	9.28 ± 0.452	8.67	9.87	8

General Description

Capital tract pins may be unsheathing. Most dorsal, humeral, crural, and femoral pins are unsheathing and have light cinnamon tips. Alar pins unsheathed 1-2 mm. Caudal pins have begun to unsheathe. Young appear alert.

General Description

All tracts are unsheathing. Capital tract beginning to unsheathe. Dorsal, humeral, and femoral tracts unsheathing significantly, giving young a soft appearance. Alar pins unsheathed by 4 - 6 mm. Apteria mostly covered by feathers and wings. Young are alert and looking around.

Day 11 Key Visual Indicators:

- Capital tract pins are significantly unsheathed
- Young appear feathered due to extent of
  unsheathing
- Young are very alert and can hop around

Feather Tract Development

Tract	N	V	P	U	F	*n*
Capital				100		8
Dorsal				100		8
Humeral				100		8
Alar				100		8
Femoral				100		8
Crural				100		8
Caudal				100		8
Ventral				100		8

Morphometric Data

Measurements	Mean ± SD	Min	Max	*n*
Weight	10.19 ± 0.476	9.5	10.8	8
Tarsus	14.33 ± 0.373	13.86	14.9	8
Wing Chord	33.5 ± 2.204	30.0	36.0	8
Culmen	5.25 ± 0.280	4.75	5.57	8
Outer Primary	17.19 ± 2.563	12.0	19.0	8
Outer Rectrix	7.63 ± 1.768	4.0	10.0	8
Longest Broken Primary	8.75 ± 1.282	6.0	10.0	8
Length	63.25 ± 3.775	58.0	67.0	4
Gape	9.10 ± 0.434	8.49	9.76	8

General Description

All feather tracts are significantly unsheathed giving
young an overall feathered appearance. Young appear
very alert, can stand upright and hop. Young are prone to
"jump"after this day. Use caution.

Literature Cited

Baldwin, S.P., H.C. Oberholser, and L.G. Worley. 1931. Measurements of birds. Scientific Publications of the Cleveland Museum of Natural History 2:1-121.

Ballard, G., G.R. Geupel, N. Nur, and T. Gardali. 2003. Long-term declines and decadal patterns in population trends of songbirds in western North America, 1979-1999. Condor 105:737-755.

Best, L.B. 1977. Nestling biology of the Field Sparrow. Auk 94:308-319.

Bize, P., N.B. Metcalfe, and A. Roulin. 2006 Catch-up growth strategies differ between body structures: interactions between age and structure-specific growth in wild nestling Alpine Swifts. Functional Ecology 20:857-864.

Boag, P.T. 1987. Effects of nestling diet on growth and adult size of Zebra Finches. Auk 104:155-166.

Briskie, J.V. 1995. Nestling biology of the Yellow Warbler at the northern limit of its range. Journal of Field Ornithology 66:531-543.

Burhans, D.E., F.R. Thompson III, and J. Faaborg. 2000. Costs of parasitism incurred by two songbird species and their quality as cowbird hosts. Condor 102:364-373.

Burns, K.J. 1993. Geographic variation in ontogeny of the Fox Sparrow. Condor 95:652-661.

Carlsson, B.-G., and B. Hörnfeldt. 1993. Determination of nestling age and laying date in Tengmalm's Owl: use of wing length and body mass. Condor 96:555-559.

Dahdul, W.M., and M.H. Horn. 2003. Energy allocation and postnatal growth in captive Elegant Tern (*Sterna elegans*) chicks: responses to high- versus low-energy diets. Auk 120:1069-1081.

Dawson, R.D., and M.T. Bidwell. 2005. Dietary calcium limits size and growth of nestling tree swallows *Tachycineta bicolor* in a non-acidified landscape. Journal of Avian Biology 36:127-134.

Dinsmore, S.J., G.C. White, and F.L. Knopf. 2002. Advanced techniques for modeling avian nest survival. Ecology 83:3476-3488.

Gill, F.B. 1994. Ornithology. W.H. Freeman and Company, New York, NY.

Geupel, G.R., and G. Ballard. 2002. Wrentit (*Chamea fasciata*). *In* A. Poole and F. Gill, editors. The Birds of North America, No. 654. Academy of Natural Sciences, Philadelphia, Pennsylvania; The American Ornithologists' Union, Washington, D.C.

Haggerty, T.M. 1994. Nestling growth and development in Bachman's Sparrows. Journal of Field Ornithology 65:224-231.

Haggerty, T.M. 2006. Sexual size dimorphism and assortative mating in Carolina Wrens. Journal of Field Ornithology 77:250-265.

Haggerty, T.M., and E.S. Morton. 1995. Carolina Wren (*Thryothorus ludovicianus*). *In* A. Poole and F. Gill, editors. The Birds of North America, No. 188. Academy of Natural Sciences, Philadelphia, Pennsylvania; The American Ornithologists' Union, Washington, D.C.

Halupka, K. 1998. Partial nest predation in an altricial bird selects for the accelerated development of young. Journal of Avian Biology 29:129-133.

Hamel, P.B. 1974. Age and sex determination of nestling Common Grackles. Bird-Banding 45:16–23.

Holcomb, L.C., and G. Twiest. 1971. Growth and calculation of age for Red-winged Blackbird nestlings. Bird Banding 42:1-17.

Jones, S.L., and G.R. Geupel, editors. 2007. Beyond Mayfield: measurements of nest survival data. Studies in Avian Biology 34.

Kilner, R.M., J.R. Madden, and M.E. Hauber. 2004. Brood parasitic cowbird nestlings use host young to procure resources. Science 305:877-879.

Kilpatric, A.M. 2002. Variation in growth of Brown-headed Cowbird (*Molothrus ater*) nestlings and energetic impacts on their host parents. Canadian Journal of Zoology 80:145-153.

King, J.R., and J.K. Hubbard. 1981. Comparative patterns of nestling growth in White-crowned Sparrows. Condor 83:362-369.

Konarzewski, M., J. Kowalczyk, T. Swierubska, and B. Lewonczuk. 1996. Effect of short-term feed restrictions, realimentation, and overfeeding on growth of Song Thrush (*Turdus philomelos*) nestlings. Functional Ecology 10:97-105.

Lack, D. 1968. Ecological adaptations for breeding in birds. Methuen, London, England.

Lepczyk, C.A., and W.H. Karasov. 2000. Effect of ephemeral food restriction on growth of House Sparrows. Auk 117:164-174.

Magrath, R.D. 1991. Nestling weight and juvenile survival in the blackbird *Turdus merula*. Journal of Animal Ecology 60:335-351.

Martin, T.E. 1992. Breeding productivity considerations: what are the apprpriate habitat features for management? Pages 455-473 *in* J.M. Hagan and D.W. Johnstone, editors. Ecology and Conservation of Neotropical Migrant Landbirds. Smithsonian Institution Press, Washington, D.C.

McCarty, J.P. 2001. Variation in growth of nestling Tree Swallows across mulitiple temporal and spatial scales. Auk 118:176-190.

Mineau, P., G.E.J. Smith, R. Markel, and C.S. Lam. 1982. Aging Herring Gulls from hatching to fledging. Journal of Field Ornithology 53:394-402.

Murphy, M.T. 1981. Growth and aging of nestling Eastern Kingbirds and Eastern Phoebes. Journal of Field Ornithology 52:309-316.

Murphy, M.T. 1983. Ecological aspects of the reproductive biology of Eastern Kingbirds: geographic comparisons. Ecology 64:914-928.

Murphy, M.T. 1985. Nestling Eastern Kingbird growth: effects of initial size and ambient temperature. Ecology 66:162-170.

Nur, N., A. L. Holmes, and G. R. Geupel. 2004. Use of survival time analysis to analyze nesting success in birds: an example using Loggerhead Shrikes. Condor 106:457-471.

O'Connor, R.J. 1978. Growth strategies in nestling passerines. Living Bird 16:209-238.

O'Connor, R.J. 1984. The growth and development of birds. Wiley-Interscience, Chichester, England.

Oyan, H.S., and T. Anker-Nilssen. 1996. Allocation of growth in food-stressed Atlantic Puffin chicks. Auk 113:830-831.

Pereyra, M.E., and M.L. Morton. 2001. Nestling growth and thermoregulatory development in subalpine Dusky Flycatchers. Auk 118:116-136.

Petersen, K.L., L.B. Best, and B.M Winter. 1986. Growth of nestling Sage Sparrows and Brewer's Sparrows. Wilson Bulletin 98:535-546.

Pinkowski, B.C. 1975. Growth and development of Eastern Bluebirds. Bird Banding 46:273-289.

Podlesak, D.W., and C.R. Blem. 2002. Determination of age of nestling Prothonotary Warblers. Journal of Field Ornithology 73:33-37.

Pyle, P. 1997. An identification guide to North American birds. Part I. Slate Creek Press. Bolinas, California.

Remes, V., and T.E. Martin. 2002. Environmental influences on the evolution of growth and developmental rates in passerines. Evolution 56:2505-2518.

Ricklefs, R.E. 1966. Behavior of young Cactus Wrens and Curve-billed Thrashers. Wilson Bulletin 78:47-56.

Ricklefs, R.E. 1967. A graphical method of fitting equations to growth curves. Ecology 48:978-983.

Ricklefs, R.E. 1968a. Patterns of growth in birds. Ibis 110:419-451

Ricklefs, R.E. 1968b. Weight recession in birds. Auk 85:30-35.

Ricklefs, R.E. 1969. Preliminary models for growth rates in altricial birds. Ecology 50:1031-1039.

Ricklefs, R.E. 1975. Patterns of growth in birds. III. Growth and development of the Cactus Wren. Condor 77:34-45.

Ricklefs, R.E. 1982. Some considerations on sibling competition and avian growth rates. Auk 99:141-147.

Ricklefs, R.E. 1983. Avian postnatal development. Pages 1-83 *in* D.S. Farner, J.R. King, and K.C. Parkes, editors. Avian Biology v. 7. Academic Press, New York, New York.

Ricklefs, R.E. 1993. Sibling competition, hatching asynchrony, incubation period, and lifespan in altricial birds. Current Ornithology 11:199-276.

Ricklefs, R.E., and S. Peters. 1981. Parental components of variance in growth rate and body size of nestling European Starlings (*Sturnus vulgaris*) in eastern Pennsylvania. Auk 98:39-48.

Ricklefs, R.E., J.M. Starck, and M. Konarzewski. 1998. Internal constraints on growth in birds. Pages 266-287. *In* J.M Starck, and R.E. Ricklefs, editors. Avian growth and development: evolution within the altricial-precocial spectrum. Oxford University Press, New York, New York.

Ross, H.A. 1980. Growth of nestling Ipswich Sparrows in relation to season, habitat, brood size, and parental age. Auk 97:721-732.

Saunders, M.B., and G.L. Hansen. 1989. A method for estimating the ages of nestling Northern Harriers (*Circus cyaneus*). Canadian Journal of Zoology 67:1824-1827.

Schew, W.A., and R.E. Ricklefs. 1998. Developmental plasticity. Pages 288-304 *in* J.M Starck, and R.E. Ricklefs, editors. Avian growth and development: evolution within the altricial-precocial spectrum. Oxford University Press, New York, New York.

Scott, T.W. 1979. Growth and age determination of nestling Brown-headed Cowbirds. Wilson Bulletin 91:464-466.

Sherry, T.W., and R.T. Holmes. 1992. Population fluctuations in a long-distance neotropical migrant: demographic evidence for the importance of breeding season events in the American Redstart. Pages 431-442 *in* J.M. Hagan and D.W. Johnston, editors. Ecology and Conservation of Neotropical Migrant Landbirds. Smithsonian Institution Press, Washington, D.C.

Starck, J.M., and R.E. Ricklefs, editors. 1998a. Avian growth and development: evolution within the altricial-precocial spectrum. Oxford University Press, New York, New York.

Starck, J.M., and R.E. Ricklefs. 1998b. Patterns of development: the altricial-precocial spectrum. Pages 3-30 *in* J.M Starck, and R.E. Ricklefs, editors. Avian growth and development: evolution within the altricial-precocial spectrum. Oxford University Press, New York, New York.

Sutton, G.M. 1935. The juvenal plumage and postjuvenal molt in several species of Michigan sparrows. Cranbrook Institute Science Bulletin 3, Bloomfield Hills, Michigan.

Walkinshaw, L.H. 1948. Nestlings of some passerine birds in western Alaska. Condor 50:64–70.

Weatherhead, P.J. 1989. Sex ratios, host-specific reproductive success, and impact of Brown-headed Cowbirds. Auk 106:358-366.

Werschkul, D.F., and J.A. Jackson. 1979. Sibling competition and avian growth rates. Ibis 121:97-102.

Appendix A.

Measurements of adults from the populations where the nestling data used in this guide was collected. Source: [1]PRBO banding records, [2]Haggerty 2006, [3]Geupel and Ballard 2002, [4]Phillips County, MT, [5]Lassen and Plumas County, CA

Species	Weight (min-max) n	Wing Chord (min-max) n	Tarsus (min-max) n	Culmen (min-max) n
Dusky Flycatcher				
Female/Male[1,5]	10.63 ± 0.75 (8.9-12.2) n = 39	66.0 ± 2.42 (62.0-73.0) n = 39	23.89 ± 0.60 (23.30-25.10) n = 12	No data
Carolina Wren[2]				
Male	21.2 ± 1.3 (18.5-27.0) n = 134	59.1 ± 1.5 (55.0-63.0) n = 14	22.3 ± 0.7 (19.5-23.8) n = 141	No data
Female	18.7 ± 5.1 (16.2-21.5) n = 118	55.3 ± 1.3 (52.0-58.4) n = 13	21.4 ± 0.7 (18.5-23.6) n = 134	No data
Wrentit[3]				
Male	15.27 ± 1.08 (12.4-18.0) n = 72	55.6 ± 1.98 (51.0-60.0) n = 74	25.4 ± 2.47 (18.0-31.7) n = 66	No data
Female	14.16 ± 1.08 (12.4-17.0) n = 43	54.4 ± 1.68 (50.0-58.0) n = 43	24.9 ± 2.28 (16.7-28.9) n = 54	No data
Sprague's Pipit[4]				
Male	23.77 ± 2.35 (19.40-31.60) n = 44	81.49 ± 2.25 (73.00-86.00) n = 51	23.85 ± 1.61 (20.00-26.78) n = 39	8.76 ± 0.78 (7.00-11.00) n = 51
Female	22.57 ± 1.78 (21.00-24.50) n = 3	76.33 ± 0.58 (76.00-77.00) n = 3	23.10 (n/a) n = 1	8.87 ± 0.32 (8.50-9.10) n = 3
Song Sparrow[1]				
Male	18.92 ± 1.21 (16.8-25.9) n = 65	59.8 ± 1.85 (55.0-65.0) n = 65	21.75 ± 0.99 (19.6-24.5) n = 65	No data
Female	17.90 ± 1.32 (13.8-23.1) n = 56	56.34 ± 2.06 (49-61) n = 56	20.95 ± 0.90 (18.5-23.0) n = 56	No data
Chestnut-collared Longspur[4]				
Male	19.75 ± 2.60 (13.60-23.90) n = 15	81.13 ± 3.30 (77.00-89.00) n = 16	20.30 ± 1.59 (18.06-22.78) n = 6	8.08 ± 0.63 (6.80-9.20) n = 16
Female	19.90 ± 0.77 (19.00-20.00) n = 5	78.25 ± 1.50 (77.00-80.00) n = 4	20.00 (n/a) n = 1	7.42 ± 0.28 (7.00-7.70) n = 5
American Goldfinch[1]				
Male	12.15 ± C 0.64 (11.0-13.8) n = 40	68.55 ± 1.66 (64.0-71.0) n = 40	No data	No data
Female	12.33 ± 1.00 (11.0-16.8) n = 79	66.05 ± 2.17 (61.0-78.0) n = 79	No data	No data

Appendix B.
Data Collection Methods and Protocols

These protocols were followed during the creation of this guide. These can be used as general guidelines by those wishing to assemble aging information for a particular study species. Templates for data sheets and a database can be found online at: www.prbo. org/tools/nestlings.

General guidelines.—When beginning to collect nestling growth data, there are several considerations to take into account. Consider how many nests are expected to be found for each species, for how many seasons data will be collected, and how much time is available for data collection. If possible, it may be a good idea to review nest-finding rates from previous seasons. This will provide an estimate of how many nests will be found before hatching. Remember that many nests will likely be found after they have already hatched. We recommend collecting data over at least a two-year period to increase sample size and because of the variability in growth that can occur between years. If only one year of data collection is possible, it may be prudent to focus on a single species in order to attain a larger sample size. Other time considerations include travel time to and from the site(s), nest accessibility within the study plot, and daily data entry.

Protocols.—Only data for young of known age should be recorded; nests found with young should not be used unless you are positive that they had just hatched (young are egg size with moist down, eggshells still in nest) or are actively hatching. Nests found before or during egg laying should be checked daily as the expected hatch date approaches. This ensures that the opportunity to measure nestlings on Day 1 is not missed and that the ability to know nestling age with certainty is not lost. In this guide, the first day that nestlings are found to have hatched is considered Day 1, even though they may have hatched during the evening. Some in the literature call this Day 0. When possible, nests should be checked in the late morning or afternoon to avoid missing the hatch date. During nest checks, eggs should be checked carefully for signs of hatching (cracked shells). Prior to approaching nestlings, a location for taking measurements is chosen and equipment prepared.

Photographs.—Photographs of nestlings add a great deal of practicality to any aging guide. Biologists out in the field can use the photos as a quick reference when finding or checking nests. Photos can also be studied before the field season begins, allowing familiarization with the appearance of young before the first nests are found. Nestlings are placed with a lateral side toward the camera on a standard light gray or non-reflective sheet of paper. A ruler showing millimeters is placed just below and parallel to the nestling. The unique ID number for each nestling and the nest day is written near the nestling. The photos are taken as close as possible to the nestlings (macro mode) while still allowing for a clear focus and inclusion of the ruler and ID. At least two photographs (often more to assure clear focus) should be taken, one vertically above and one along the nestling's profile. Before taking photographs, be sure you are comfortable and familiar with your camera. Pay attention to lighting conditions. When using macro mode on the camera, pay particular attention to its focusing abilities and depth of field range.

Equipment.—Clipboard, data sheet, background sheet (for photographs), pens, non-toxic permanent marker (or string), electronic calipers, small ruler, wing rule, electronic scale, camera, cloth bird bag.

Precautions.—Precautions should be taken to minimize disturbance around a nest. When possible, nestlings should be measured within a similar time window each day, avoiding the early mornings or late afternoons, which are critical feeding periods. Nestlings should be kept away from exposure to direct sun or winds, and monitored closely and returned to the nest if their health seems at risk (heavy panting, shivering, wet conditions). Nestlings should not be measured during very hot, cold, or wet days. We found that two to three nestlings in relatively accessible nests could be measured and photographed within about 20-25 minutes of being removed. If it is taking any longer than this, measurements should be taken in priority order as time allows (See "Variables used for aging" above).

Removing and returning nestlings.—Nestlings should be visited daily, or every other day if daily visits are not possible. If the latter, measurements for some nests should begin at day two. Alternatively, if sample size allows, nest visits can be staggered between nests, making sure to attain data from each nest day. Young are placed in a cloth bag and transported outside of the parent's territory. All young are collected initially, but only two are marked and measured from each nest. These two are selected from the bird bag during the first visit by simply reaching into the bag and using the first two nestlings reached. In subsequent visits, it is only necessary to remove these two marked individuals from the nest. In some cases, however, it may be easier to remove the entire brood during each visit. In a few cases, marked nestlings disappeared from the nest. In these cases, a third nestling of known age may be marked and measured from that point on. Nests with older nestlings should be approached cautiously to help prevent premature fledging. When older nestlings are replaced, a hand can be kept over them until they settle down to help prevent premature fledging. It is best to use great caution or not measure them after this point.

Nestling identification.—Nestlings are marked on toenails or toes on a specific foot (left or right) or with a specific color using a non-toxic permanent marker, or by tying a short loose colored string around the leg (excess string trimmed). In many cases nestlings may need to be re-marked on a daily basis to ensure accurate identification. Each nestling is given a unique ID, with the following data: species (AOU code), plot, nest number and attempt, marked foot (L or R), and year (e.g., BAIS G2 11A L 2004 for a Baird's Sparrow from plot G2 nest #11 attempt A marked on the left foot and measured in 2004). This is written on the top of all the data sheets for each individual, and nest age should be included on each photograph as noted in Fig. B-1.

AGE	SPECIES	PLOT	NEST #	FOOT	YEAR
1	BAIS	G2	11A	R or L	2004

Fig. B-1. An example of systematic labeling of data sheets and photographs which uniquely identifies each nestling and their age.

Banding Young.—When banding nestlings is one of the study objectives, nestlings should be banded at an appropriate time to avoid injury or premature fledging prior to banding. For many species feather development, along with behavioral clues, are usually accurate enough alone to guide time of banding. The unsheathing of the alar pins may coincide well with the first day a nestling can be banded safely (i.e., proper leg size for bands). Note that nestlings that are handled may fledge sooner than normal (Pereyra and Morton 2001).

U.S. Department of the Interior
U.S. Fish & Wildlife Service
Route 1, Box 166
Shepherdstown, WV 25443

http://www.fws.gov

October 2007